Superbikes

of the seventies

Superbikes

of the seventies

John Nutting
Motor Cycle

DOMUS BOOKS

First published in the United States in 1978 by
Domus Books
400 Anthony Trail
Northbrook
Illinois 60062

ISBN: 0-89196-022-8

Library of Congress Catalog Card Number: 78-3146

Filmset in England by Photocomp Limited, Birmingham
Printed in Hong Kong

Contents

Introduction

Superbikes are the pinnacles of manufacturers' development; demonstrations of technological prowess; objects of fantasy and worship; expressions of individuality.

Superbikes have never been so wonderfully diverse as they are today. Whether it is on six-cylinder tarmac rippling sportsters, water-cooled tourers, threes, flat twins, vee-twins or sophisticated fours, the modern motor cyclist can find instant freedom and exhilaration when he rides off on his impressive steed.

Yet it is only a decade since the first real superbike appeared, Honda's CB750 four. Japan showed the way, exploiting the thirst for one-dimensional American travel. Power was – and is – what Americans wanted and that first brilliant effort provided the impetus for others, Britain, Italy, Germany and America, to follow.

The common thread is engine size and power. Ten years ago the best bikes were good for 120 mph; the fastest now can comfortably top 140 mph and rip through the standing quarter-mile in under twelve seconds.

Nevertheless, a second generation of superbikes is appearing. While pleased that such stunning machines existed at all, European motor cyclists regarded first with amusement an later with scorn the poverty of handling associated with the early superbikes; they were fine in straight line but lamentably wobbly when ridde enthusiastically on twisty continental roads.

The manufacturers recognised this basi shortcoming and achieved new heights of all round sophistication. Not only do the secon generation bikes corner well but maintenance i simplified, with shaft drive and strong engines

The tenth anniversary of the superbike will b seen too as the year the capacity race started Kawasaki started with their 1,015 cc Z1R four Yamaha replied with a 1,101 cc shaft drive doh four, Laverda opened out their dohc three t 1,115 cc and Honda introduced a 1,047 cc six.

Despite murmurings of discontent from thos who regard the superbike as a wasteful indu gence in money and metal, it is here to stay Factories see it as a necessity to explore th higher levels of performance, if only to sho their competitors and buyers alike of thei capabilities, for this can reflect on other mach ines in their ranges.

There is nothing illusory about a superbike. shamelessly displays engineering design in one c

Three of the most recent additions to the superbike line up:
Right: *from Italy is the 1,115 cc version of the Laverda's twin overhead camshaft three, the 1200.*
Far top: *the fastest and most powerful roadster ever offered for sale, the six-cylinder Honda CBX, which develops 103 bhp at 9,000 rpm for a top speed over 140 mph.*
Far lower: *the shaft drive Yamaha 1100*

...e few easily attainable fusions of man and
...achine.

This book covers twenty of the best superbikes
...hat have appeared in a decade. Outright per-
...ormance is not the only criteria, and while many
...f the bikes were good in their day they have been
...clipsed by later machines; nevertheless they
...layed a part in the development of the super-
...ike.

Readers will find some machines missing, the
...atest because they are so new, others because
...hey simply did not become available for a full
...est. The collection here has been ridden, tested
...nd enjoyed in the course of preparing road test
...eports for *Motor Cycle*; the texts of these tests
...ave been updated to put each machine into
...erspective.

I have had the pleasure to ride all the bikes,
...ut I am indebted to Bob Currie and Stewart
...oroughs for use of their test material, to Dave
...ichmond for picture research and Don Morley
...or the provision of colour photographs.

Bikes that are super have always existed, but
...he word was coined as recently as 1968.
...herefore *Superbikes of the Seventies* is a
...ollection which covers the best of that decade.

JAN

Note: The specifications of the machines covered
...n this book have differed slightly from market to
...market.

7

BMW R100RS

BMW, for so long steeped in a traditionally conservative approach to building motor cycles, have never been regarded as pacesetters. After all the German company has been successfully making bikes since 1923 and the principles that resulted in the latest range of 980 cc models are just the same as they were 55 years ago; that their goals of simplicity, refinement and good handling could be best served by the air-cooled, horizontally-opposed twin with shaft drive.

On the face of it then, the R100RS is a radical departure from the BMW mould. Initially, the striking appearance of the R100RS's streamline body work hints of a new direction in the Be Emm camp. Certainly it is true that few man facturers have succeeded in selling a fully faire machine. And there is no doubt that the BMW R100RS is a pacesetter. For it raises the state the 'art' in motor cycle aerodynamic design to new level. In fact, the R100RS is the logica progression of BMW's basic concept of offerin machines which are peerless long-distance cru sers; the fairing merely enables the rider to rais this ability to new levels, levels which are now fa

bove that offered anywhere else.

Even without the fairing, the biggest of the BMW twins are superlative machines for touring: light, economical and breathlessly relaxed at speed. Exploiting the slim shape to tuck the rider in, BMW have always offered the standard of riding comfort, like the quietness of the exhaust, by which others are judged. The addition of the 'cockpit' merely raises this standard to a new high. With the R100RS, the rider can now enjoy covering massive distances at 100 mph or more and still arrive at his destination fresh. In bad weather he remains dry and clean.

Riding the bike is at first an uncanny experience. The streamlining is so well integrated that the rider never feels aware of it until he glances down at the speedo and realises that he is travelling at 100 mph when he thought he was doing a relaxed 60 mph.

The difference between this and other motor cycle streamlining intended for road use is based in the initial BMW concepts. It is not made for increased speed; had this been the aim they would have used a much lower profile. What they wanted was to insulate the rider from wind pressure while using the normal riding stance, and use the fairing to provide a degree of aerodynamic downthrust to improve the stability at high speeds, the lack of which was becoming embarrasing on the R100S version of the 980 cc twin with its small handlebar screen.

Using the Pinifarina wind tunnel in Italy BMW achieved just those aims.

To all intents and purposes BMW have created a bike that behaves just like any other solo – but has none of the problems that make a mockery of the performance claims of the competitors. Although many other bikes can easily better 125 mph, in real practical terms this is virtually impossible because of high handlebars and awkward footrests.

With the claimed power output of the R100RS engine, 70 bhp at 7,250 rpm, in mind, our top speed figures may be considerably lower than expected. The mean two-way top speed of 113·8 mph obtained at MIRA is slower than many seven-fifties, and the standing quarter mile time of 14·2 seconds is lower than the unfaired R100/7 BMW. But it has to be remembered that these figures were taken with the rider sitting upright, and then the true picture comes to light – on most other unstreamlined bikes this would be almost impossible! And that top speed can be maintained without tiring the rider as long as there is fuel in the tank.

The other advantages of the fairing are immediately apparent whether you ride the R100RS slow or fast. In town at relatively modest speeds the screen still protects the rider from the weather as well as offering a bright object for other road users to see. And the handling is perceptibly more stable at speeds over 50 mph. BMW claim that the wedge shape of the screen and the spoiler either side give 17 per cent extra downthrust compared to the naked machine.

BMW also claim a six per cent cut in drag. While this shows as a bonus in top speed if the rider remains sitting upright (if he crouched down on the naked bike he would go faster still), the main advantage is one of improved fuel economy.

Cruising at a steady 100 mph, the R100RS returned 35 mpg, which combined with the capacity of the 6·3 gallon tank offers the rider a range of at least 200 miles. Most other bikes at this speed would be struggling to better 25–30 mpg with ranges of half the Bee-Emm's.

At a more casual (and legal in the UK) 70 mph, the benefits are even more startling. At this speed the bike returned 48 mpg! But the most was made of the RS's long leggedness and our overall test consumption over 1,300 miles was 36·8 mpg including the MIRA tests and some commuting.

The only drawback of the addition of the fairing is its weight. With it the R100RS weighs in at over 500 lb (although this is still less than most smaller seven fifties) and the flat out acceleration takes a dive.

The R100RS engine, unlike its Japanese competition, is remarkably unsophisticated. A simple pushrod opposed twin with very over-square dimensions (94 × 70·6 mm), it is lower, flexible and light. And with a massive flywheel very sweet in use. Only mechanical noise is the tapping of the valve rockers.

Specification

Engine: 980 cc (94 × 70·6 mm) overhead valve, horizontally-opposed flat-twin. Light-alloy cylinder head and barrels; cast-iron liners. Two plain main bearings; plain big ends. Wet sump lubrication with Eaton-type pump and replaceable paper oil filter. Compression ratio, 9·5 to 1. Two 40-mm choke Bing constant-velocity carburettors with cable-operated cold-start jets; paper element air filter. Claimed maximum power, 70 bhp at 7,250 rpm. Maximum torque, 55·7 lb-ft at 5,500 rpm.

Transmission: Crankshaft-mounted single-plate dry clutch. Helical gears to five-speed gearbox. Overall ratios: 13·2, 8·58, 6·27, 5·01 and 4·5 to 1. Shaft final drive (ratio, 3 to 1 with optional 2·91 to 1).

Electrical Equipment: Coil ignition. 12-volt, 28-amp-hour battery and 240-watt field-excited alternator. 7·5-in diameter headlamp with 60/55-watt quartz-halogen main bulb. Five fuses in headlamp.

Brakes: Cable and hydraulically-operated 10·25-in diameter twin perforated disc front, 7·87-in drum rear.

Tires: Metzeler, 3·25 × H19-in ribbed front, 4·00 × H18-in patterned rear. Light-alloy rims.

Suspension: Telescopic front fork with adjustable steering damper. Pivoted rear fork with three-position manual multirate spring preload adjustment.

Frame: Welded duplex cradle with oval spine and bolted-on rear subframe.

Dimensions: Wheelbase, 58·5 in; seat height, 32·5 in; ground clearance, 6·5 in; overall width, 29·5 in; trail 3·5 in; turning circle, 17 ft 10 in; all unladen.

Weight: 511 lb including approximately one gallon of fuel.

Fuel Capacity: 6·3 gals including 8·4 pts reserve.

Sump Oil Capacity: 4·8 pts.

Manufacturer: Bayerische Motoren Werke AG, D-8000 Munchen 80, West Germany.

Performance

Maximum Speeds (Mean): 113·8 mph; 111·4 mph with rider in oversuit sitting normally.

Best One-way Speed: 115·9 mph – dry track, slight tail wind.

Braking Distance – from 30 mph: 27 ft 6 in.

Fuel Consumption: 36·8 mpg.

Oil Consumption: negligible.

Minimum Non-snatch Speed: 14 mph in top gear.

Speedo Accuracy:

Indicated mph	30	40	50	60	70	80	90
Actual mph	27·4	36·6	45·8	55·3	64·8	75·5	86·1

The main attraction, however, of the R100RS engine is its flexibility, even though it is the most highly tuned of the three 980 cc flat twins in the BMW range. It is this flexibility which makes the bike one of the most formidable on the road.

Once into top gear on the five-speed gearbox, there was rarely any need to change down unless coming to a stop, even in town. Solid torque is delivered from 2,000 rpm, and although the power unit is not one of the smoothest the bike leaps forward with the slightest throttle opening.

Mid-range pick-up is where the R100RS scores best and this is demonstrated most impressively in top gear acceleration from 50 mph.

Compared to say, the super sports Honda CB750F, which over the standing quarter is over a second quicker, the R100RS accelerates like a rocket from 50 mph in top, and although the Honda catches up slightly as it hits its power band it fails to make up the initial loss.

Nevertheless the R100RS is not perfection from stem to stern, for of its high-speed touring role, where it is incomparable, it can be uncomfortable.

To allow the fairing to be narrower, the handlebar is shorter and slightly lower than on the other BMWs; this throws more weight onto the rider's wrists, and it can be tiring when the bike is ridden in town for any length of time.

There are also a couple of annoying vibration periods which, although they do not detract from the high level of comfort, annoy because they stand out against the general standard of sophistication.

First, torque pulse vibration occurs when opening up at low revs, and can only be minimised by very careful synchronisation of the carburettors. There is also a period of resonance between 80 and 85 mph which renders the mirrors useless. Fortunately, the clarity of the mirror images is restored at 100 mph.

The gearchange in the three higher ratios is silent and slick, but equally noiseless changes in the lower gears still call for a co-ordination of controls, particularly in the stop-go of city traffic.

Otherwise the response to the controls is impeccable. The black hand levers, by Magura, are well contoured for comfort and the clutch is light and smooth with a wide contact point. The throttle has considerably less movement than on earlier BMWs, yet retains a light action. The Hella switchgear is improved, with longer thumb switches for the dip and indicator.

BMW roadholding and handling has always been very good and the steering is top notch thanks to the forward-mounted axle contributing to low inertia around the steering axis, an aspect improved further by moving the headlight into the fairing.

Even with a fractionally larger turning circle the R100RS can still be turned feet up in the average road width.

Changes have been made to the suspension, some good, some bad. The long, soft action is retained, although the front fork has slightly

ronger springs than the R100S to counteract
he downward thrust created by the stream-
ning. The rear units have multi-rate springs for
optimum ride comfort with a variety of loads.

In fast going over bumpy roads, the bike
andles superbly with an uncanny combination
f ride quality and directional stability. In the
et, the Metzeler tires give safe and predictable
rip without a sudden breakaway.

However, when ridden more sedately, the
100RS shows the other side of the coin.
xcessive seal friction and heavy compression
amping in the front forks virtually lock up the
ront suspension over short sharp bumps like pot
oles and manhole covers. In a short ride in
own, the RS reveals none of the luxury qualities
hat you would expect of it. It is very much a bike
hat has to be ridden hard and fast to appreciate
s best qualities. Although attractive and im-
ressively styled to match the fairing the one plus
half RS seat is of little use in day to day riding,
eing too short to accommodate any but the
mallest of passengers; the S seat offered on the
978 models as standard is more sensible. Under
he lockable seat are a bin for bits and pieces plus
he toolkit trough and, in the nose of the seat
adding, a first aid kit. A rubber-covered security
hain is hidden up inside the main frame tube.

Finished in dusted silver with blue lining with
old as an option, the R100RS has superb
aintwork.

Quality of construction shows a singularly
ncompromising attitude to design that is
ypified by the use of tapered and oval tubing for
he frame, exceptionally powerful and reliable
lectrics with a searing halogen headlamp and a
nassive 28-amp-hour battery, plus a pair of
tunning Fiamm air horns. The electric starting is
s reliable as ever. Appreciation of the need for
asy maintenance is shown by the quickly
etachable wheels and a centre stand that is at
he balance point of the bike.

The brakes and wheels too are of the highest
quality. For 1978, the rear drum brake was
eplaced with a perforated disc similar to the pair
itted to the front wheel. All three discs are
extremely progressive in action and work better
han most in the rain. Wheels are now the Italian
nade cast-alloy units originally shown on the
977 prototypes.

Such are the details that push the price well
bove the norm but contribute to a refined and
ractical machine.

With Honda, Moto Guzzi and Yamaha
ffering shaft-drive 1,000 cc touring machines
vith dazzling performance figures there is plenty
f choice for the mega-buck touring rider. But
nly BMW still offer a machine that is really
lifferent and practical for high speed use as well
s having that touch of quite exclusivity.

Few things compare with the thrill of charging
omfortably and unobtrusively through the
ight behind the cosy glow of the instruments in
he cockpit, the time on the quartz clock seeming
o slow down with the way the R100RS can
ompress the miles.

*Cockpit view of the
R100RS shows the
instrumentation; speedo
and rev counter plus a
voltmeter and quartz
clock in the top of the
fairing*
*Far left: accessibility to
the flat twin engine is
not hampered by the
fairing*

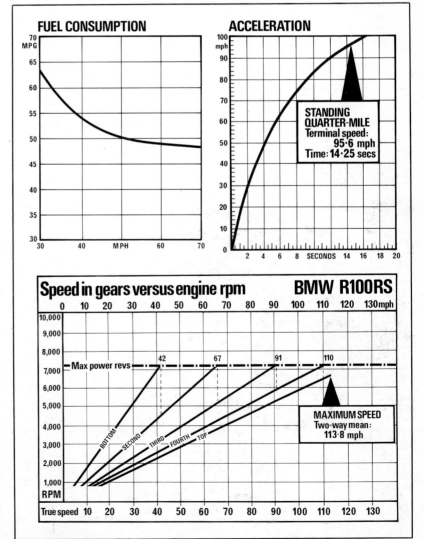

FUEL CONSUMPTION

ACCELERATION

STANDING
QUARTER-MILE
Terminal speed:
95·6 mph
Time: 14·25 secs

Speed in gears versus engine rpm   **BMW R100RS**

Max power revs   42   67   91   110

MAXIMUM SPEED
Two-way mean:
113·8 mph

BOTTOM SECOND THIRD FOURTH TOP

Ducati 860 GTS

As far as their objectives of fine handling and usable road performance are concerned, Ducati have always had their priorities right. Few manufacturers have been able to equal the combination of flexibility and smoothness offered by Ducati's vee-twin engines. Their record in such demanding races as the Barcelona 24-hours at the round-the-houses Montjuich Park is testimony enough to the quality of the Ducati's steering and roadholding.

Lamentably, however, poor detail finishing and electrical equipment has given Ducati a reputation for rough quality that will take a long time to wear off.

The Ducati 860 GTS, introduced in 1976, wa the first indication that the factory was able t offer a machine finished to the same level as th Japanese. It was based on the Guigiaro-style 860 GT that had proved to be so impractical o the road. The GTS was offered with a mor sensible seat and tank and makes a much mor agreeable tourer.

Like all the big Ducatis, the 860 GTS has th vee-twin engine so loved by purists of moto cycle design. Being a 90-degree engine, it offers pleasant lack of vibration and a slim profile tha allows the unit to be slung low in the frame for low centre of gravity.

The frame itself is sensibly made of straight tubing and incorporates the engine as a part of the structure. Triangulated and very strong, it offers tremendous rigidity from the use of thick-walled tubes – a feature that, while it may add a few pounds to the overall weight of the machine, more than offsets this with Ducati's almost legendary high speed handling.

Drawbacks of the Ducati approach to its engine design are that the complexity of the bevel and shaft drive to the overhead camshafts make it notoriously expensive to machine and assemble. Fans of the distinctive mechanical melodies made by such a layout will however be pleased to know that the costs of redesigning the valve gear with quieter toothed belts, as on the more recent 500 cc vee-twin, are far greater in the long run than the current production costs and we shall be able to have the pleasure of riding the 860 vee-twin Ducatis for some time yet.

Another drawback of the Ducati approach to the vee-twin is that its length limits the minimum length of the machine. With a wheelbase of exactly 5 ft, the Ducati 860 GTS is one of the longest machines of its type. While conferring a degree of stability during cornering rarely experienced on other machines, such a feature detracts from the bike's manoeuvrability at low speeds and requires a greater angle of lean for a given cornering speed. This means that any clearance advantage offered by the narrow width of the engine unit is more quickly eaten up. As a result, the frame and suspension limits are rarely approached.

Ducati have persevered through the eight years since the first 750 cc models were introduced. In 1974, the 864 cc version with a bore and stroke of 86 by 74·4 mm was introduced with newer styling for the crankcases and the option for an electric starter.

Demand for a more practical big bore Ducati as an alternative to the Super Sports desmodromic production racer led to the 860 GTS and the more recent 900 Darmah, which has the desmo valve gear of the sportster but with a softer state of tune and more up-to-date styling with Japanese instrumentation and cast magnesium wheels.

The 860 GTS is nevertheless a good balance between specification and price, being offered at substantially less than the Darmah. The most obvious difference between the GTS and its predecessors is the fat fuel tank with a 4·8-gallon capacity. There is also the low and wide seat. Instrumentation was taken from the obsolete 750 Sport with the British Smiths' clocks mounted on an alloy plate with the ignition lock between them.

The electronic ignition fitted to the first eight-sixties meant that the kick starter had to be given a hefty swing to fire up the bike, a very awkward task with the kick starter so close to the footrests. But the electric starter, which is mounted atop the primary gearcase with the relay under the nearside side cover and connected by a rod to the engaging gears, makes starting easy. It is just a matter of lifting the mixture enrichening lever and punching the little button on the left handlebar console.

Once running, everything that made the old sports singles like Velocettes so appealing – a classical and unique blend of mechanical sound and a broad road flexibility – is recalled on the Ducati. Its road performance is superb. While not immensely powerful compared to many 900 cc or 1,000 cc bikes, tractability and low-end punch of the Ducati makes the bike a daunting competitor on twisty and demanding roads. Snapping open the throttles of the 32-mm choke Delorto carburettors is rewarded by an instant kick in the back and this happens whether riding through town or whistling along the open road. The top speed of 103 mph with the rider sitting upright is comparable to many bigger machines.

Although the bike has an excellent five-speed gearbox, with a very pleasant change mechanism, there is very little reason to use it. Once into top gear there is hardly a circumstance which requires changing down. Even baulking by slower traffic at motorway speeds is seldom frustrating, as with a twist of the right hand the big vee-twin surges forward with hardly a hiccup.

Like many similar flexible bikes, the performance is never shown up to apparent advantage in the absolute performance figures. The addition of improved intake silencing and exhaust pipes which emit a deep drone has chopped the top end torque to the degree that there is no reason to rev

the unit beyond 6,500 rpm, although Ducati quote the maximum power of around 60 bhp at 7,000 rpm. The weight has crept up too. At 520 lb the 860 GTS is the heaviest ever from the Bologna factory. This shows in the slower quarter mile time of 13·85 sec, with a terminal speed of 97 mph.

The test bike had also had its overall gearing lowered by an extra tooth on the rear wheel sprocket. This gave a top gear ratio of 5·04 to 1 and while improving the mid-range response at around 70 mph it lowered the bottom gear ratios to a level that made it difficult to prevent near-uncontrollable wheelspin during standing starts, which lost additional time.

For the state of tune of the Ducati, it mean that it was revving at an unusually high 4,70 rpm at 70 mph. Flat out in top gear with the ride flat on the tank at a mean 114·9 mph the engine was revving well over its power peak, at 7,70 rpm. It is possible that Ducati geared th machine with a normally seated rider in mind but it is also certain that the bike would hav been much faster through the timing lights wit higher gearing and would probably have bee quicker through the quarter mile.

On the positive side though was the shee pulling power of the GTS. Hills would b flattened with hardly any throttle movement while at the test strip, it accelerated from 40 mph to 92·5 mph in top gear in a quarter mile, the bes figure for that test ever recorded for any bike.

Ninety-degree vee-twins are appealing fo their perfect primary balance. In practice, how ever, the bigger the engine gets, the bigger are th secondary forces; in the case of the Ducati thes act at approximately 35 degrees from the hori zontal and at twice the frequency of the engin revs. At high speed this is shown by a buzz through the handlebar and footrests, but it onl became bothersome at around 5,000 rpm.

Fuel consumption was improved compared with the GT version, by about 2·5 mpg; this wa possibly due to the slightly higher compression ratio of 9·8 to 1. Using premium fuel, the GTS returned 35·9 mpg overall, dropping to 31·6 mp at the test strip while up to 39·1 mpg was possible with careful riding. Oil consumption was mini mal – just as well, as the filler plug at the front o the sump is the worst encountered for undoin and topping up.

Ducati are one of the few manufacturers who offer footrests with height adjustment. Se properly they give the Duke a comfortable riding position to 85 mph although the new, lower dua seat lacks padding enough for a comfortable rid over 100 miles. For a vee-twin the Ducat footrests are surprisingly wide at 27 inches tip t tip, and this produces a cornering clearanc problem.

The very strong frame and taut steering of th GTS encourages brisk bend swinging and th footrests can be worn down very easily withou riding hard. The footrests can be raised easily bu this produces an awkward riding position.

This is despite very stiff suspension. Shor travel Ceriani front forks are used, but these ar not comparable in quality to some Cerianis we have experienced. Chattery over ripples, they lacked the lithe feel normally associated with Italian suspension.

To lessen the effects of the long wheelbase radical steering geometry with a 60½ degree hea angle and a massive 5 inches of trail are used. Th effect is to make the steering extremely taut a speed but heavy around town. Plenty of physica force is needed to swing the bike through shar bends and a degree of precision that leaves littl room for mistakes when riding fast.

Fortunately the big Metzeler tires were ve grippy in the dry, in strong contrast to thei

---

Specification

Engine: 864 cc (86 × 74·4 mm) overhead camshaft, 90° vee-twin. Light-alloy barrel and heads; cast-iron liners. Three ball main bearings; needle-roller big ends. Wet sump lubrication; gear pump. Compression ratio, 9·8 to 1. Two 32-mm choke Delorto carburettors with accelerator pumps and cable-operated cold-start jets; paper element air filters. Claimed maximum power, 67·7 bhp at 7,000 rpm. Maximum torque, 61 lb-ft at 4,000 rpm.

Transmission: Primary helical gears (ratio, 2·187 to 1). Wet, multiplate clutch and five-speed gearbox. Overall ratios: 12·7, 8·88, 6·84, 5·68 and 5·04 to 1. Final drive by 0·625 × 0·375-in chain (ratio, 39/15). Mph at 1,000 rpm in top gear, 14·9.

Electrical Equipment: Electronic ignition. 12-volt, 32-amp-hour battery, 200-watt alternator and voltage regulator. 7-in diameter Aprilia headlamp with 60/55-watt quartz halogen main bulb. Four fuses.

Brakes: Brembo 11-in diameter double disc front with double-acting calipers, 7·875-in diameter drum rear, cable operated.

Tires: Metzeler, 3·50 × H18-in block C66 front, 120/90 × H18-in block C88 rear.

Suspension: Ceriani telescopic front fork. Pivoted rear fork with Marzocchi dampers with five-position spring preload.

Frame: Welded duplex tube type incorporating engine unit.

Dimensions: Wheelbase, 60·25 in; ground clearance, 7 in; seat height, 31·25 in; handlebar width, 28 in; castor angle, 60·5°; trail, 4·9 in; turning circle, 15 ft 2 in; all unladen.

Weight: 520 lb including one gallon of fuel.

Fuel Capacity: 4·9 gals including 2·4 pts reserve.

Sump Oil Capacity: 7·8 pts.

Manufacturer: Ducati Meccanica SpA, Via A. C. Ducati, 3, Cas. Postale 313, 40100 Bologna.

Performance

Maximum Speeds (Mean): 114·9 mph; 102·8 mph with rider in two-piece outfit sitting normally.

Best One-way Speed: 118·7 mph – dry track, 5 mph three-quarter tail wind.

Braking Distance – from 30 mph: 30 ft 10 in.

Fuel Consumption: 35·9 mpg.

Oil Consumption: Negligible.

Minimum Non-snatch Speed: 24 mph in top gear.

Speedo Accuracy:

Indicated mph	30	50	60	80
Actual mph	27·8	47·4	59·4	81·5

British instruments are used on the Ducati 860 GTS with below the dials a row of light-emitting diode warning lights
Far right: drawback of the Ducati vee-twin layout is the arranging of the air filters. Above the swinging arm pivot is the relay for the starter and its connecting linkage

parently poor wet grip; a problem that was racked down to misaligned wheels. On most her bikes this can be corrected at the rear-wheel ain adjusters, but the Ducati has eccentric ljusters at the swinging arm mount which eclude anything but frame straightening.

Double discs are now offered on the GTS front heel and the power provided is phenomenal. In ct these brakes were so powerful that the 30 ph stopping distance tests revolved around a ick to prevent the front wheel locking.

The rear drum was merely average by com- rison. It faded in normal use and was insensi- ve in an emergency.

The Ducati's electrics are a vast improvement previous models. The transistorised ignition is aintenance free and the voltage control unit for e massive 32-amp-hour battery is electronic o. The 60-watt quartz-halogen headlamp sends t a strong, safe beam that is ideal for quick ght riding. Only the awkward hand switches id the microscopic light-emitting diode warn- g lamps spoil the electrics.

The tools, which sit in a plastic tray under the ckable seat are adequate for most of the tasks quired, but the spanners were brittle and broke used clumsily.

Faults were confined to a speedo that failed wards the end of the 700 mile test and some rrosion on the main fuse that blacked out the ke. There was no prop stand but the main stand as easy to use.

The Ducati 860 GTS has such a pleasing aracter that grows on you that owners find it sy to ignore the poor chrome and soft paint st for that thundering silky urge of the big vee- in with the cantering exhaust note.

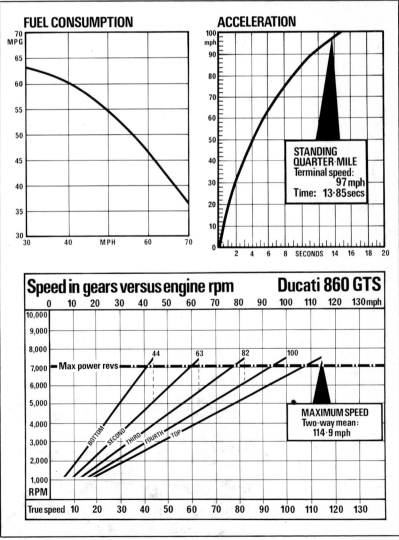

FUEL CONSUMPTION

ACCELERATION

STANDING
QUARTER-MILE
Terminal speed:
97 mph
Time: 13·85 secs

Speed in gears versus engine rpm　　**Ducati 860 GTS**

Max power revs

BOTTOM　SECOND　THIRD　FOURTH　TOP

MAXIMUM SPEED
Two-way mean:
114·9 mph

Harley-Davidson FXE-1200

There is nothing quite like gunning down the highway at 70 mph on a big Harley-Davidson vee-twin. Perhaps it is the overwhelming presence of the vast engine churing around at a lazy 3,250 rpm or perhaps it is the rangy, built-like-a-truck feel that is so appealing. Either way, there is something instantly attractive about a motor cycle that almost seems alive.

It rumbles, it cranks, it clatters and it vibrates – but what motor cycle retaining any connection with the grass roots of two-wheel travel didn't? Or so the Harley buff's argument goes. Therein lies the reason *why* there is nothing quite like a Harley – other makers have seen fit to bring wider appeal to their bikes by modern design and refinement. Meanwhile Harley-Davidson remain staunchly in the traditionalist's camp with their 20-year-old design in the biggest of their vee-twins, the FXE-1200.

All the same, riding a Harley-Davidson is a unique experience. For a start, you do not so much ride the bike but sit in it, the saddle being somewhere at axle height and the controls somewhere about 3 ft above it. And no sooner have you sunk into that deep saddle than you start scowling and snarling at your fellow road users. The Harley is that *bad*, and the other guys had better know it.

Fantasies, however, last only so long, and all the imagery in the world cannot cover up the fact that the Harley is rough and, in the case of the FXE1200, over-priced when looked at realistically.

The twelve-hundred engine is the bigger of the two Harley-Davidson 45 degree vee-twins and famous for powering the romantic FLH1200 Electra-Glide tourer. The Super Glide is the cut-and-shut version, a lighter (if 585 lb with a gallon of fuel can be called light), leaner and more esoteric machine with its western droop 'bars, 3-gallon tank, banana seat and abbreviated fenders. There is one concession to civility, signified

y the E suffix in the FXE-1200 model number, nd that is the electric starter, a necessity if you refer riding to sweating up a lather by the side of he road. But even the starter motor is in haracter. Switching on with the ignition lock idden between the cylinders and applying just a mall amount of choke, the mechanism grinds nto action and the motor bursts into life with a umplety-rumplety exhaust note which, thanks the latest style exhaust system, is muted very fectively.

The rest of the machine is still pure vintage, owever. The result is that the exhaust system everely reduces the performance as well.

Harley-Davidson claim a maximum power utput of around 65 bhp at a leisurely 5,500 rpm, ut the actual power fell far short of this in test nd the best we could extract out of the bike at IIRA was a two-way mean speed of 108 mph, nd a best run of almost 114 mph. Flat-out cceleration, too, is hardly in the superbike class ith a standing quarter-mile time of 15·3 econds. Not that this matters too much on the ad. For the redeeming feature of the FXE is orque – mountains of it. Right from the outset e modestly tuned 1,207 cc engine makes it bvious that it does not need to be rushed to rovide the goods. With the peculiar Bendix arburettor (now replaced by a Japanese Keihin quivalent), which acts more like an on-off witch at small openings, the reaction to a tweak f the grip from low revs is instantaneous and nonumental.

As a rule, 2,500 rpm was more than enough to aintain a clear road ahead through the four-peed gearbox and even for modest cruising, as ese revs corresponded to over 50 mph in top ar.

This was just as well, since vibrations start in

earnest at 3,200 rpm, buzzing the instruments frantically, and only marginally smoothing out towards the rev limit at 6,000 rpm. The happiest cruising speed was at 3,500 rpm, where the chugging motor had plenty in hand for instant overtaking.

Despite the laid-back feel of the bike, its crudity cannot be overlooked. In addition to the rough carburation and painful vibration, the transmission is poor, with only a tough damper on the crankshaft to take up the shocks, and the suspension is hard. You ride the Harley in a series of bangs and clanks. The non-unit gearbox has a linkage-operated one-down, three-up lever, and while much better than the box on the Sportster XL-1000 it still shows its age. Neutral is easy to find, but the unit is clonky, most gears dropping into place with the caress of a pile-driver.

In contrast, the dry clutch in a massive alloy casting is perfect. Light in action, the take-up is so smooth that slipping it at low speed to cover up the snatching transmission is easy.

By reputation, Harley handling is pretty foul, but we found the steering very good on the FXE. The low engine and riding position makes the bike very easy to flick through bends, although the lack of ground clearance, even with the rear suspension units jacked up to the highest pre-load, leads to a grinding side stand and footrests in corners.

Longer than the Sportster, the riding position takes some getting used to, but with the deeply-padded seat is comfortable, the only real critic-ism being the way the hands tend to slip off the downward-angled and smooth grips.

The hard suspension, weak frame and slippery tires lead to the main handling faults on the FXE-1200. Both front and rear spring travel is

short and the lack of rigidity in the frame can cause the bike to get out of shape easily. Bumpy corners mean plenty of action for the rider. In the wet the Goodyear tires indicate forcefully that they were never intended for greasy roads. Pulling away from stops in the rain is a balancing act between traction of the big 5·10 × 16-in rear tire and throttle opening.

Although disc brakes are used at the front and rear, they continue the theme of crudity. Both brakes are powerful enough to lock the wheels,

Specification

Engine: 1,207 cc (87·3 × 100·8 mm) overhead valve, 45° vee-twin. Light-alloy cylinder heads and cast-iron barrels. One double-roller, one single-roller main bearing with outrigger bush on timing side. Dry sump lubrication; gear pump. Compression ratio, 8 to 1. One 38-mm choke Bendix carburettor with accelerator pump and plunger-operated choke; foam-mesh air filter. Claimed maximum power, 65 bhp at 5,500 rpm.

Transmission: Duplex 0·5 × 0·31 in primary chain. Dry, multiplate clutch and non-unit four-speed gearbox with direct top gear. Overall ratios: 10·25, 6·24, 4·21 and 3·42 to 1. Final drive chain, 0·625 × 0·375 in. Mph at 1,000 rpm in top gear, 22.

Electrical Equipment: Coil ignition with single contact breaker, 12-volt, 18-amp-hour battery, 300-watt alternator with electronic voltage control. 5·5-in diameter headlamp with approximately 55-watt sealed-beam unit. Starter motor; thermal circuit breakers.

Brakes: Hydraulically operated 11·75-in diameter chromed-steel disc front, 9·75-in diameter disc rear. Floating calipers.

Tires: Goodyear MM90 3·50 × 19-in. ribbed front, MT90 5·10 × 16-in. rear studded.

Suspension: Telescopic front fork, 3·5 in travel. Pivoted rear fork with three-position spring preload adjustment.

Frame: Duplex loop cradle with cast lugs.

Dimensions: Wheelbase, 61·75 in; ground clearance, 6 in; seat height, 29 in; footrest height, 11 in; handlebar width, 29 in; turning circle, 14 ft 6 in.

Weight: 585 lb including one gallon of fuel.

Fuel Capacity: 3·3 gals including 7·2 pts reserve.

Sump Oil Capacity: 8·4 pts.

Manufacturer: Harley-Davidson Motorcycles, 3700 West Juneau, Milwaukee, Wisconsin 53201.

Performance

Maximum Speeds (Mean): 108·3 mph; 100·4 mph with rider seated normally in oversuit.

Best One-way Speed: 113·8 mph – dry track, slight tail wind.

Braking Distance – from 30 mph: 30 ft 3 in.

Fuel Consumption: 31·7 mpg.

Oil Consumption: 580 mpp

Minimum Non-snatch Speed: 18 mph in top gear.

Speedo Accuracy:

Indicated mph	30	40	50	60	70	80
Actual mph	26·2	35·7	45·4	56·5	66·3	76·1

but the calipers rattle badly, the rear unit tending to grab as well. The controls do not help. Like the clutch, the reach on the front-brake hand lever is excessive and the rider needs to lift his foot off the rest to reach the rear brake.

Fed by a massive alternator mounted behind the primary drive on the crankshaft, the electrical system is modern enough but suffered from silly faults. The size of the headlamp (5½ in), belies the power of the sealed unit which throws a healthy spot main and wide dipped beam. But the battery capacity is too low and plenty of night use meant that the engine failed to spin over on the button next morning. Also, chafed ignition wires which shorted out demonstrated the use of the thermal contact breakers, which reconnect the supply when the fault is corrected.

The indicators are operated by press buttons

on either handgrip, a very unsatisfactory method when you have to manipulate the other controls at the same time. On the good side, the stentorian horn is fabulous. You not only hear it but feel it too, it's so powerful.

Only a prop stand is fitted, but it does have a locking mechanism to prevent the machine rolling away on a slope.

In general use, the FXE-1200 Harley does not show up as well as the Sportster. Fuel consumption never varied much from the 33 mpg and, indicating a poor setting-up of the carburettor, the steady speed fuel consumption readings hardly varied between 30 mph to 70 mph.

Oil leaks from the chaincase and the pushrod tubes contributed mainly to the heavy oil consumption of 580 miles to the pint. In practice, the oil tank is replenished from the small dipstick hole on the side as the seat needs to be unscrewed for access to the main cap, and no tools are supplied.

This does not sound very promising, but the reasons why someone should spend a large sum on such a machine are varied anyway. Perhaps the magic moment when you charge out of a 50 mph bend, change into top at 2,500 revs, and chug off into the horizon in a dream is one of them!

Rider's view of the handlebar shows the big rubber mounted grips and button-operated direction indicators Below: there is no mistaking the 1,207 cc 45 degree vee-twin. Inside the big transmission cover is a dry clutch driving a four-speed gearbox

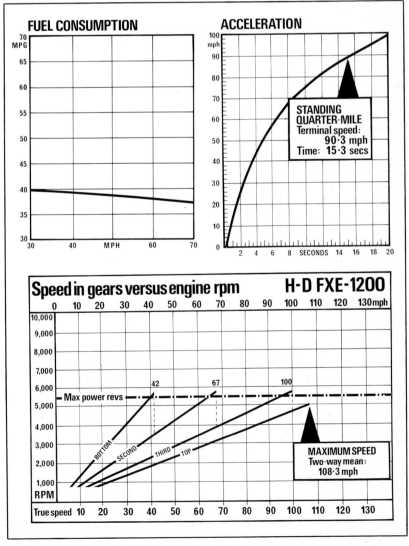

FUEL CONSUMPTION

ACCELERATION

STANDING QUARTER-MILE
Terminal speed: 90·3 mph
Time: 15·3 secs

Speed in gears versus engine rpm   **H-D FXE-1200**

Max power revs   42   67   100

BOTTOM   SECOND   THIRD   TOP

MAXIMUM SPEED
Two-way mean:
108·3 mph

Harley-Davidson XLCR-1000

Black power hit the roads of America when Harley-Davidson's cafe racer XLCR-1000, originally shown as a styling exercise in 1974, was put into production three years later. It was a radical departure from the Harleys that built a legend, but it was every bit as exciting as its menacing midnight looks promised. Claimed by the Milwaukee factory to be the fastest road-going bike they had ever produced, the XLCR is a bike in the European mould, nimble as a cat and slim as a dart. Yet underneath it is pure Harley. Wind on the fat twistgrip and the 61 cubic inch vee-twin motor rumbles you forward with all the latent power of a steam locomotive.

Can the XLCR catch on in America, its home?

If the Florida scene around Daytona 200 time i any reflection of the Stateside trends then, afte their brief excursion into the limelight in the mid 1970s, cafe racers with their rear-set footrest and back-breaking racing crouch riders are a much a minority interest as ever.

There are hordes of choppers. And touring bikes are almost universal, decked out in ar identical manner with Vetter touring fairing enclosing the tape deck and CB radios and enough luggage gear to dwarf a Cadillac American mainstream motor cycling mean covering hundreds of miles on ruler straigh highways or cruising down to the shopping mal for a couple of six packs. Neither encourage th

e of tricked-out racing equipment.

But in Europe the XLCR is a complete change from the normal Harleys – which are low, bulky and agricultural. It has a new appeal to the rider who spends more time on – and revels in – twisty roads.

Although it has plenty in common with the chopper-style Harleys, the XLCR feels like a Sportster should feel – responsive and nimble, and the antithesis of an Electra-Glide.

It was originally designed by Harley's Director of Styling, William G. Davidson, brother of the President, John A. Davidson. He based it on the front half of a 1,000 cc Sportster engine and frame and mounted on the rear the back end of the XR750 dirt track racer with its longer swinging arm and more vertical suspension units. A small black tank and solo racing seat almost straight off the racer, complemented by a BMW-style top half fairing on the handlebar, completed the bodywork.

The cycle parts were given all the looks of modern racing tackle. Wheels are seven-spoke light-alloy castings by Morris. Brakes are double discs on the front wheel and a single on the rear, all operated by floating calipers. Tires are the latest sports covers by Goodyear, in wide 3·75 and 4·25 profiles on 19-in front and 18-in rims respectively.

Chugging through Daytona Beach the XLCR felt decidedly alien, much more like a European machine than the usual Harley-Davidsons that we have become used to. The racing style riding

position is remarkably comfortable. You lean forward over the sculptured tank and grip a straight handlebar. The seat with its press-studded cover is deep enough to keep the aches away. And the footrests are mounted so that the weight is placed evenly on all the contact points.

The controls are pure Harley though. The grips are fat and smooth and the hand levers, while very effective and handy, look like hand carved alloy. Switchgear, too, is bulky and crude and retains the novel but awkward press buttons on each console for the direction indicators.

As on the 1977 bikes, the gearchange is on the 'Japanese' left side with a reverse lever, while the rear-brake lever is a massive forging of unbreakable proportions that looks as if it was liberated from a truck chassis; it operates the rear disc through a Kelsey Hayes master cylinder.

For boulevarde cruising the XLCR is pleasant enough. At moderate speeds the steering has a light and neutral feel that makes the bike a natural bend swinger. And with such massive punch at low revs the engine encourages a relaxed approach without using the gearbox. But if you attack your riding with more verve, the bike takes on a different character as it is pushed harder through bumpy or fast bends.

The suspension is by the Japanese Kayaba factory and compares both in appearance and performance with the sort of equipment found on Japanese bikes of the early 1970s, in other words, not very impressive.

The XLCR is stiffly sprung as well as offering a

large degree of resistance to the absorption of tarmac seams and joins, both of which spoil the comfort and the handling. The flimsy rear fork does not contribute greatly to the overall stability, as the bike bounces along the road with the usual Harley oblivion to the more sophisticated needs of today's motor cyclist. The vibration, too, becomes more than normal

mortals can usually bear over more than half a hour of riding.

Like all Harley-Davidsons, the focal point of the XLCR is its massive vee-twin engine. Unchanged in general specification from the XLC Sportster, the 45-degree twin has a charm all of its own, which is more than a little influenced by the vintage appearance of the cast-iron cylinders and heads. Bore and stroke are very under square, in contrast to current trends, with dimensions of 81 by 96·8 mm for an overall swept volume of 997 cc. In Harley tradition, the cylinders are mounted on crankcases that contain crank flywheels of monstrous dimensions and the connecting-rod big ends are not side-by side, but have a split rear big end that encases the front one. The big overhead valves are pushrod operated with the carburettor between the cylinders.

Concessions to modern practice are unit construction and electric starting; in fact the one-time ritual of firing up the beast is removed entirely as there is no kick starter. What electrical components there are prove to be as massive as ever, with a solid looking dynamo nestling between the front cylinder and splayed frame tubes and a bulky battery over the clutch housing. Special for the XLCR are hand-finished and carefully assembled power units. These are tested for power and the more potent examples are sidelined for use in the XLCR series, the rest going back to the Sportster line.

Harley-Davidson claim a maximum power of 61 to 62 bhp at 6,200 rpm for the standard engines so this is more than likely to be exceeded by the XLCR units. Whatever it is, Harley-Davidson give the bike a 12-month and 12,00

Specification

Engine: 997·5 cc (81 × 96·8 mm) overhead valve, 45° vee-twin. Cast-iron heads and barrels. Dry sump lubrication. Compression ratio, 9 to 1. Keihin 38-mm choke carburettor with accelerator pump; paper element air filter. Claimed maximum power, 61 bhp at 6,200 rpm. Maximum torque, 52 lb-ft at 3,800 rpm.

Transmission: Primary triplex chain. Wet, multiplate clutch and four-speed gearbox. Overall ratios: 10·63, 7·7, 5·82 and 4·22 to 1. Final drive by 0·625 × 0·375-in chain. Mph at 1,000 rpm in top gear, 18.

Electrical Equipment: Coil ignition. 12-volt battery and dc dynamo. 6-in diameter headlamp with 45/35-watt main bulb. Starter motor; direction indicators; overload circuit breakers.

Brakes: Hydraulically-operated 10-in diameter duplex disc front, single disc rear.

Tires: Goodyear Eagle A/T, 3·75 × 19-in front, 4·25 × 18-in rear, on cast-alloy wheels.

Suspension: Kayaba telescopic front fork. Pivoted rear fork with five-position spring preload adjustment.

Frame: Duplex tube cradle with cast lugs.

Dimensions: Wheelbase, 58·5 in; seat height, 31 in; handlebar width, 27 in; ground clearance, 8 in; all unladen.

Weight: 520 lb.

Fuel Capacity: approximately 3 gals.

Manufacturer: Harley-Davidson Motorcycles, 3700 West Juneau, Milwaukee, Wisconsin 53201.

Performance

Maximum Speeds (Mean): 115 mph (estimated); 100 mph (estimated) with rider normally seated.

Best One-way Speed: 115 mph (estimated).

Fuel Consumption: approximately 37·5 mpg overall.

Oil Consumption: approximately 420 mpp.

Minimum Non-snatch Speed: 15 mph in top gear.

ile warranty. Also new for the 1977 Harleys ere Keihin carburettors made by the same firm at supplied Honda. The carburettor is a replica f the old simple Bendix unit with a single rottle valve and a massive choke button rrouting from the side.

Pull this, prime the combustion chambers om the carb's accelerator pump with a couple f twists of the grip, punch the big starter button n the handlebar and the big twin rumbles into e with its classic off-beat exhaust note from the ack silencers.

From there on riding the bike is just a matter f letting the torque do the work. The clutch is eavy and the gearchange labourious so that nce you snick into the highest of the four speeds ere is rarely any need to change down, unless ou stop at a light.

The overall gearing is very low with top gear ving just 3,900 rpm at 70 mph, a speed at which e Harley is no more than idling along. Tweak e grip and the bike, although fairly heavy at 20 lb, immediately kicks forward.

Through the four gears, flat out acceleration is isk, but it is ragged and seems quicker than it ally is. Nowadays a quarter-mile time of about 3 sec is only average for a 1,000 cc sports bike. The top speed of 115 mph is similarly none too npressive, although faster than any other arley made for the road. More pertinent owever is the manner in which the performance offered. Swinging through bends with the little otrests kissing the road, the syncopated note of e exhaust rebounding off the sidewalls, the LCR becomes at one with the image that its opearance suggests. Such is the mystery and arm of such a machine, not the cold facts.

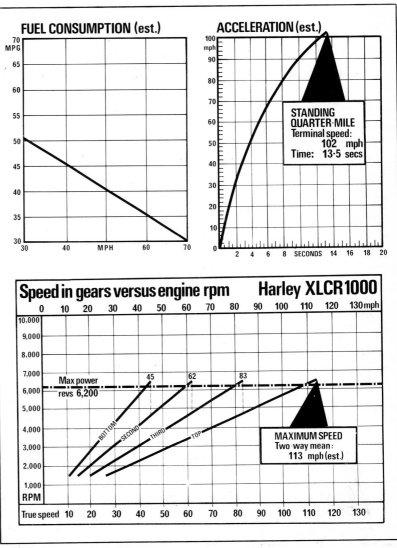

FUEL CONSUMPTION (est.)

ACCELERATION (est.)

STANDING QUARTER-MILE
Terminal speed: 102 mph
Time: 13·5 secs

Speed in gears versus engine rpm   Harley XLCR 1000

Max power revs 6,200

MAXIMUM SPEED
Two-way mean: 113 mph (est.)

Honda CB750F2

Honda never let the grass grow under their feet. Quick to respond to changes in the market, as soon as their Super Sports 750 cc four was upstaged in performance and looks by Suzuki's GS750 four in late 1976, they quickly unveiled a new and even more potent model, the CB750F2.

The CB750F1 had been a positive effort by Honda to appeal to the purely sporting rider. Sharp styling and performance were allied to frame improvements to offer more stability at high speeds. It was the first effort by Honda in six years to change the image of a machine that had remained largely conservative in appearance since it started the superbike boom in 1969.

Menacingly resplendant with its all-black paintwork and engine set off by the five-spoke composite construction wheels based on the designs first used on the factory 1,000 cc

endurance racers, the CB750F2 takes the sports theme further. Basically unchanged since it was introduced, the 736 cc overhead camshaft four-cylinder engine retains the same bore and stroke (61 × 63 mm) and the ruggedly reliable transmission with duplex primary chains taking the drive to the multiplate clutch and five-speed gearbox. Unusual by contemporary standards is the use of a countershaft behind the gearbox to take the drive to the final-drive sprocket.

For the F2, a retuning boosts the power and increases the rev band of the unit. Taking care of the higher power output is a heavier pitch endless rear chain with sealed links to improve life. Nevertheless, there are marks on the rear-wheel spindle mountings showing the amount of movement permissable before replacement is necessary. To marginally update the handling

d high speed cornering stability there is new
steering geometry, altered suspension settings
and a tidier four-into-one exhaust system with
greater ground clearance.

Where the F1 was capable of just over 120
mph, the F2 is a genuine 125 mph machine – and
looks it. Equipment is first class. Mounted on the
'Comstar' wheels, which have stiff pressed-steel
spokes and rolled light-alloy rims bolted to the
hubs, are two brake discs at the front, with the
single piston calipers mounted behind the fork
legs, and a large diameter disc at the rear.

For night riding, the headlamp is a powerful
quartz halogen unit, and there are two equally
impressive horns mounted either side of it.

The 1976 CB750F1, the engine of which is now
used in the same trim in the CB750K7, produced
bhp at 8,500 rpm. The CB750F2, by stretching
the upper rev limit, gives more . . . 70 bhp at
9,500 rpm. This has been achieved by installing
bigger valves and fitting the camshaft with a
different profile. Inlet-valve sizes are increased
from 32 to 34 mm, the exhausts from 28 to 31
mm, with stiffer springs (increased from 154 to
172 lb/in) to prevent valve float at the higher revs
used. The long stroke motor can now be safely
revved to over 10,000 rpm through the gears.

The larger valves called for a different valve
angle and consequently there has been reshaping
of the porting and of the combustion chamber,
and a slight lowering of the compression ratio to
prevent a broken marriage between the valves
and pistons.

Looked at from a speed for speed's sake
viewpoint the power boost produces the results.
The bike takes off smoothly with a sharply
determined power band starting at 6,000 rpm
and goes like a jet up to the end of the rev
counter's red sector, 10,500. The mean top speed
of 124·6 mph reached is over 2 mph up on the F1
and puts the F2 up alongside its 1,000 cc
stablemate, the GL1000 Gold Wing, in a flat-out
catch race. Given good conditions, the
CB750F2 goes even better; with a tail wind it
clocked a best speed of over 128 mph!

For everyday use, a marginal increase in valve
clatter on tickover and a loss in tractability can
be set against the power increase. For despite the
drop in overall gearing (down to 5·51 to 1)
minimum non-snatch speed of the F2 in top gear
17 mph. The more flexible F1 accelerates
more strongly in top gear and more cleanly from
little over half that speed.

The loss shows in the standing quarter-mile
times, too. The F1 zipped through at 13·2
seconds with a terminal speed of 100·9 mph.
Despite more power and lower gearing the best
we could get from the F2 was 13·5 seconds (but
terminal speed was improved to almost 102
mph).

Feeding in the clutch and keeping the revs up
give the best result. Fitted with 242 lb/in springs
in place of the 220 pounders used in 1976, the
clutch withstood the punishment well and better
than some earlier tests with 750 Honda engines
when swelled plates necessitated adjustment.

Another contributory factor to the slower
quarter-mile times is extra weight. For with the
additional disc and caliper, horn, heavier duty
chain and other modifications, weight is increased by 25 lb over the F1 tested in 1976.

Honda make amends with extra comfort and
better fuel economy on the F2.

For the first time on a Honda 750 four,
carburettors with enclosed lifters are used. Of the
same choke size as the old models, 28 mm, the
Keihin units sport accelerator pumps that allow
the use of leaner overall jetting.

Pottering along at a steady 30 mph (33
indicated) the F3 returned a best figure of 66·6
mpg. Overall we averaged 37·7 mpg, an improvement on 1976. Provided the revs were used, the
engine was quite happy on regular fuel; but
lugging it below 5,000 rpm revealed a tendency
for pinking.

The front fork, with a softer spring rate and
modified damping valve arrangement, is the
most comfortable and forgiving Honda have
produced for the 750s so far, and with the new
rear shocks few will find fault in the model's
handling. This can become hairline at speed, but
with nearly $4\frac{3}{4}$ inches of trail the steering is
inevitably heavy and slightly cumbersome in
filtering up to 20 mph through traffic. With the
same frame as the F1, the F2 handlebars flutter
slowing down through the 40–35 speed bracket,
but there is little cause for concern. Few but cafe
racers will find the need for further ground
clearance with the four exhausts tucked neatly
away into the high-mounted chrome
silencer – one of the few items to escape the
black paint treatment.

The silencer is particularly effective and makes the exhaust inaudible over the loud gearbox whine in third, fourth and top.

Going to the other extreme are the twin horns; this is a component regularly criticised by road testers in the past, irrespective of the make or model, but now it is changing. The effectiveness, by doubling up, has improved by leaps and bounds and the pair on the F2 made even the rider jump on the odd occasion they were needed.

Similarly the brilliant Stanley halogen 60/65 watt headlight offers laser-like power compar to the older offerings. Set correctly, the sharp c off on dip prevents any chance of glare dazzli oncoming drivers or riders, while the vee-bea illuminates the kerb yards further ahead f safety. Once you have ridden at night behind t Honda's headlamp, or equivalent, you real just what you are missing when you ride wi second-rate equipment.

To cope with the extra power, and aiming fo longer life, a heavier duty $\frac{3}{4} \times \frac{3}{8}$-in endless dri

Specification

Engine: 736 cc (61 × 63 mm) single-overhead camshaft, transverse, in-line four. Five plain main bearings; plain big ends. Dry sump lubrication with trochoid pump; oil filter. Compression ratio, 9 to 1. Four 28-mm choke Keihin carburettors with accelerator pumps and cold-start flaps; paper-element air filter. Claimed maximum power, 70 bhp at 9,500 rpm.

Transmission: Duplex primary chain. Wet, multiplate clutch and five-speed gearbox. Overall ratios: 14·22, 9·72, 7·58, 6·45 and 5·51 to 1. Spur gears and endless 0·75 × 0·375-in drive chain (ratio 14/43).

Electrical Equipment: Coil ignition. 12-volt, 14-amp-hour battery and 210-watt alternator. 7-in diameter headlamp with 60/55-watt Stanley H4 quartz halogen main bulb. Starter motor; direction indicators; headlamp flasher and three fuses.

Brakes: Hydraulically-operated dual 11-in diameter stainless-steel disc front; single 12-in diameter disc rear.

Tires: Bridgestone 3·25 × H19-in ribbed front; 4·00 × H18-in patterned rear.

Suspension: Telescopic front fork. Pivoted rear fork with five-position spring preload adjustment.

Frame: All welded, duplex cradle.

Dimensions: Wheelbase, 58·75 in; seat height, 32·5 in; ground clearance, 6·5 in; handlebar width, 28·5 in; castor angle, 62°30'; trail, 4·69 in; turning circle, 17 ft; all unladen.

Weight: 515 lb including one gallon of fuel.

Fuel Capacity: 4·8 gals.

Oil Capacity: 7·2 pts.

Manufacturer: Honda Motor Co. Ltd., 27-8, 6 Chome, Jingumae, Shibuya-ku, Tokyo.

Performance

Maximum Speeds (Mean): 124·6 mph; 108·4 mph with rider sitting normally.

Best One-way Speed: 128·4 mph – dry track, light tail wind.

Braking Distance — from 30 mph: 28 ft 3 in.

Fuel Consumption: 37·7 mpg overall.

Oil Consumption: Negligible.

Minimum Non-snatch Speed: 17 mph in top gear.

Speedo Accuracy:

Indicated mph	30	40	50	60	70	80	90	100
Actual mph	26·9	36·0	45·1	54·3	63·5	74·3	83·6	94·4

Honda's long standing four-cylinder single overhead camshaft CB750 sported 'Comstar' wheels with pressed-steel spokes and light alloy rims for 1977. Engine power was boosted to 70 bhp at 9,000 rpm with new carburettors, camshaft and larger valves

...ain replaces the former $\frac{5}{8} \times \frac{3}{8}$-in chain. Each ...aring is packed with grease at manufacture ...d sealed in by rubber O-rings. It is very ...ective and only needed re-tensioning by a third ...a turn of the spindle adjusters in 600 test miles. ...The F1 with its single disc was never short on ...opping power, and braking is even more ...pressive with the F2's two discs on the front ...eel. Sensibly each stainless-steel disc is thinner ...an the single, to help save unsprung weight, ...d the calipers are mounted to the rear of the

fork reducing the steering inertia. Disc pads, the same all round, are now slotted to improve wet weather performance.

With a stopping distance from 30 mph of 28ft 3in, the tires now handicap stopping in even shorter distances – with such a potent front brake the tire loses adhesion without much provocation. With the nose pinned down the rider should tread lightly on the rear brake, for if anything the new 12-in diameter disc is too much brake for the job.

The Comstar wheels, so radically different from spoked or cast-alloy jobs, meet with immediate approval. They are very strong, suit the concept and enhance the looks of the F2 – if anything they are progressively winning over their opponents as they become more familiar and accepted. Setbacks, if you approve of their looks, are poorer accessibility for cleaning between the five 'spokes' compared with the cast-alloy type; and similarly they cannot be trued like a normal spoked wheel after a minor shunt.

With little bright relief offered by a maroon petrol tank and side panels, it is up to the wheels, chromed exhaust, clutch and contact-breaker covers, and alloy generator cover, to provide contrast. This Honda have achieved with boldness and taste on the F2.

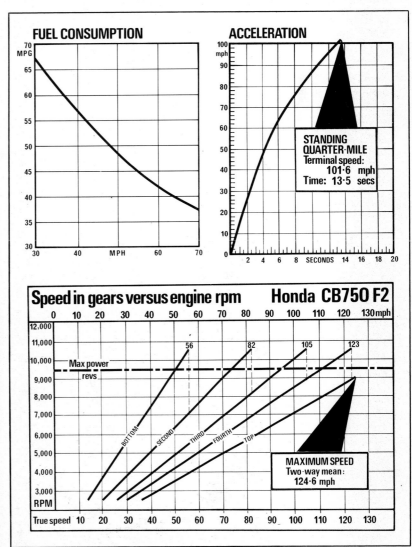

FUEL CONSUMPTION

ACCELERATION

STANDING QUARTER-MILE
Terminal speed: 101·6 mph
Time: 13·5 secs

Speed in gears versus engine rpm   Honda CB750 F2

Max power revs

BOTTOM   SECOND   THIRD   FOURTH   TOP

56   82   105   123

MAXIMUM SPEED
Two-way mean: 124·6 mph

Honda Gold Wing GL1000

If there is one machine that typifies American motor cycling and the fact that it is essentially different from biking in Europe it is the Honda Gold Wing. Without justification, this has been described as a two-wheeled tank, or more mildly as a car without bodywork. In fact few bikes can equal the Gold Wing for luxurious high-speed cruising.

It was designed with the Stateside tourer expressly in mind. What he wanted was a bike that could cover massive mileages without trouble on the open freeways that span the North American continent. He wanted a machine that could carry enormous amounts of luggage as well as a passenger.

Few bikes, if any, could satisfy Americans completely in these aspects. Those which were offered were often unreliable or expensive. What

Honda introduced in 1974 was the biggest a heaviest machine ever marketed by the Japane company. And it was the bike that the America wanted. Utterly quiet, as smooth as silk a trouble free with its shaft drive, it came at a pri that undercut the opposition by as much as per cent. It was an immediate success. It was al a revolutionary motor cycle.

Barely a couple of years earlier, nobody wou have thought that soon there would be a wat cooled horizontally opposed flat four on t market at a price that anybody could afford. B here it was, and it was not the monster th everybody expected.

Honda had to make the machine manageab at low speeds, or it could have been a comple flop, so they designed the bike with the conce tration of heaviest parts as low as possible in t

ame. To this end the gearbox is beneath the crankshaft, a bonus being that the engine is shorter too. Helping to reduce the centre of gravity, the fuel tank is mounted under the rider's seat, the dummy tank being used to house the air filter, the electrics, the overflow tank for the engine coolant and a small tool tray. Remarkably, the bike steers very well and is a lot more manageable than one might expect of a machine weighing 650 lb with a full tank, which is almost 200 lb more than the Kawasaki Z1000. Despite its bulk and very high gearing it is surprisingly fast for what is basically a touring bike.

It has of course been pushed out of the limelight by more recent big machines from Yamaha and Suzuki, but no machine has been able to give the feel of the iron fist in the velvet glove as effectively.

From idling revs to 8,000 rpm the power is developed in a smooth continuous stream. The only vibration, and it could hardly be called that, exists when you shut off or when pulling hard from a walking pace in top gear.

The impression of speed, since the only sounds the engine makes are muted clicks and whines, comes from wind pressure and roar.

Cruising at 100 mph is completely natural for the Gold Wing. It whistles along with plenty in hand and with total stability. Theoretically, the bike is capable of 140 mph on the top gear ratio of 4·5 to 1. But this is really too high and, in practice, the actual top speed is around 125 mph as we found at our MIRA tests. Straight line acceleration is stunning too, and the Wing's 80 bhp at 7,500 rpm gently wafts you to over 60 mph in 4 sec and 100 mph in a shade over 13 sec. The

lazy sounding engine achieves this with a distinct lack of commotion. Apart from the four 32-mm choke carburettors between the crankcases and the dummy tank, it has more in common with car power units than bike engines.

The four 72-mm cylinders (stroke is 61·4 mm) have wet liners and are pressed into the two halves of the crankcases which are split vertically. Light-alloy cylinder heads have offset valves and overhead camshafts driven by toothed belts from the front end. The left-hand camshaft also drives the contact breaker, while the fuel pump is driven by the right-hand camshaft.

Cleverly, the 300-watt alternator is gear-driven from the crankshaft so that its opposed motion offsets the in-line crank and minimises the reaction when the revs rise and fall quickly.

Transmission from the crank is by a Morse-type chain to the wet, multiplate clutch (a very sensitive unit that dislikes excessive slipping) and the slick and crisp-acting five-speed gearbox. An idler gear takes the drive to a spring torsion damper and the drive shaft inside the right-hand fork leg to the rear wheel and spiral-bevel gears.

Inevitably, the first impression of the machine is its overwhelming bulk. The wheelbase is 61 inches and if the dummy tank were real it would hold at least 8·4 gallons. But the seat is low, if a little hard, and reaching the ground with the feet is easy for any but the shorter rider.

Pulling the car-type choke button next to the speedo and rev counter and pressing the starter button next to the twistgrip immediately has the engine running at 3,000 rpm from cold. No juggling with the throttle is called for as the

The Honda Gold Wing's water-cooled flat four owes more to car practice than motor cycles. The overhead camshafts are driven by toothed belts and the gearbox is beneath the crankshaft.
Far right: electrics, air filter and a tool tray are inside the dummy tank. The rear fuel tank is under the seat

Specification

Engine: 1000 cc (72 × 61·4 mm) overhead camshaft, water-cooled, opposed flat four. Light-alloy cylinder heads, steel linered cylinders integral with crankcase. Three plain main bearings; plain big ends. Wet sump lubrication. Compression ratio, 9·2 to 1. Four 32-mm Mikuni constant-velocity carburettors with handle-bar operated cold start flaps; paper element air filter. Claimed maximum power, 80 bhp at 7,500 rpm.

Transmission: Inverted-tooth primary chain. Wet, multiplate clutch and five-speed gearbox beneath crankshaft. Overall ratios: 11·98, 8·18, 6·39, 5·25 and 4·5 to 1. Final drive by reduction gear from layshaft and cardan shaft. Mph at 1,000 rpm in top gear, 17.

Electrical Equipment: Twin coil ignition. 12-volt, 18-amp-hour battery and contra rotating, 300-watt alternator and voltage regulator. 7-in diameter Lucas headlamp with 60/55-watt halogen bulb. Direction indicators; starter motor; water-temperature gauge; electric fuel gauge; headlamp flasher.

Brakes: Hydraulically-operated 11-in diameter duplex disc front, 11·5-in diameter single rear.

Tires: Dunlop Gold Seal, 3·50 × H19-in ribbed front, 4·50 × H17-in studded rear. Light-alloy rims.

Suspension: Telescopic front fork. Pivoted rear fork with five-position spring preload adjustment.

Frame: Duplex tube with pressed-steel gusseting and removable left-hand side bottom rail for engine access.

Dimensions: Wheelbase, 60·5 in; ground clearance, 6 in; seat height, 31·5 in; overall length, 91 in; turning circle, 17 ft; all unladen.

Weight: 616 lb.

Fuel Capacity: 5 gals including 7·2 pts reserve.

Sump Oil Capacity: 7·4 pts.

Manufacturer: Honda Motor Co. Ltd, 27-8, 6 Chome, Jingumae, Shibuya-ku, Tokyo.

Performance

Maximum Speeds (Mean): 124·6 mph; 111·4 mph with rider in two-piece outfit sitting normally.

Best One-way Speed: 130 mph — dry track, strong tail wind.

Braking Distance — from 30 mph: 29 ft.

Fuel Consumption: 34·6 mpg.

Oil Consumption: negligible.

Minimum Non-snatch Speed: 17 mph in top gear.

Speedo Accuracy:

Indicated mph	30	40	50	60	70	80	90	100
Actual mph	29·2	39·5	49·7	58·7	67·8	77·6	87·4	97·2

complex choke mechanism opens the flaps shade to keep the revs steady.

The engine is ready for work almost instantl The pressurised water-cooling system warms u quickly with the aid of a thermostat and within few minutes the needle of the temperature gaug in the rev counter face creeps to the bottom of i range.

From then on the only attention the bea requires is regular refilling with fuel. Despite i weight, the Gold Wing can be economica particularly as it runs on the cheapest grade fuel. Over 1,000 miles of testing it averaged 3 mpg, with a slightly better consumption o motorways.

This gives a range of about 145 miles befor the fuel gauge on the top of the dummy tan shows empty, giving roughly 40 miles more o the 7·2 pint reserve capacity. Ideally, a bike lik this should have a range of 200 miles befor running onto reserve.

The riding position is acceptable, although no in the BMW class because of the excessive reac to the handlebar.

Given the Gold Wing's market, its handling beyond criticism. Ridden in the reserved fashio that one would expect of a tourer, it corner steadily if with a slight 'fall-in' effect under 3 mph and is manageable in traffic, more so tha many European machines. But it is not sporting machine and if ridden as such will bit the rider hard, which is why the Wing ha received so much criticism from Europeans.

The fold up footrests are very low and like th enormous exhaust system that wraps around th rear wheel, are easily scraped on the road whe cornering briskly.

The suspension is harsh too, detracting from the ride quality at normal cruising speeds, and the damping is less than adequate when the bike is pushed hard through bumpy bends. There are things that cannot be done with a 650 lb motor cycle, and it cannot be made to feel like a lightweight when the pace gets hot. The rider must remember that he has very little room for maneuovre when riding fast.

Wet weather riding shows up some good and some bad features of the bike. Riding at speed, the rider is well protected from water spray by the well valanced front mudguard and cooling radiator. But the brakes are not well protected – normally, the stoppers, two front stainless steel discs and one rear, are powerful and progressive, but in wet weather, particularly at slow speeds in town and when drenched on motorways, the discs lack any sort of bite at all. The only recourse for the rider is to dab the brakes periodically to keep them dry. Hopefully Honda will soon have an answer to this braking problem.

The electrical system is up to the usual standard expected from Honda and enhanced by the powerful quartz halogen headlamp.

The Gold Wing is a sensible and cheaper alternative to the 980 cc BMW twins. In a straight line it is probably better and the gear change on the Honda is definitely superior. The quality of construction that dictates the higher price of the BMW is reflected only in better handling, appearance and durability. The same goes for the Guzzis which also have shaft drive.

The competition will take a long time to come up with a bike as good as the Honda at the same price.

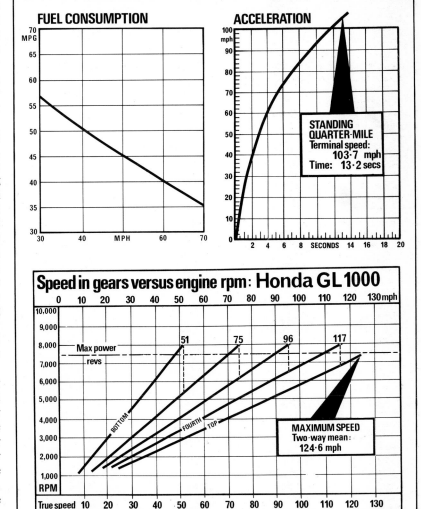

FUEL CONSUMPTION

ACCELERATION

STANDING
QUARTER-MILE
Terminal speed: 103·7 mph
Time: 13·2 secs

Speed in gears versus engine rpm: Honda GL 1000

Max power revs

BOTTOM   FOURTH   TOP

MAXIMUM SPEED
Two-way mean:
124·6 mph

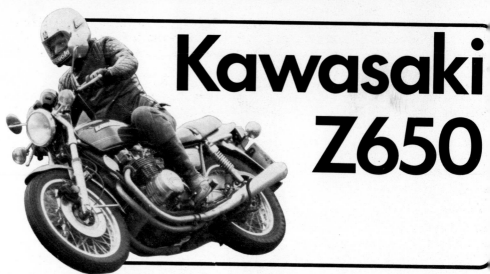

Kawasaki Z650

Kawasaki's Z650 four has carved itself an enviable reputation for speed and stamina since it appeared in late 1976. Proof of the speed came at Daytona in the following March when Kawasaki attacked the world 750 cc endurance records with a trio of mildly modified Z650 roadsters. They came away with a bunch of records that would have been impressive for a 1,000 cc roadster, let alone a 650. Best were the FIM world 1,000 km at 128·4 mph, the AMA/FIM six-hour at 127·7 mph and the AMA 100-miler at 130 mph. For good measure they rounded off with the world FIM 24-hour record at 117·2 mph. Earlier, the American, Rich Willet attacked the round the coast Australia record on his Z650 with a colleague. Just over ten days later he was back at Sydney having covered 9,550 miles to beat the record for the toughest trip in motor cycling by the scant margin of one hour. This was despite the 44-year old St Louis

businessman spending a day helping his com panion to hospital after a crash and after side swiping a kangaroo hard enough for Rich to thin he had broken a leg. The Z650 never missed a bea

We were not quite so adventurous during ou own 600-mile road test but we learned that thos records were no fluke. Firstly, there is no doub that the Z650 is very fast. It can accelerate to 6 mph as quick as anything you can buy on wheel If proof was ever needed that there is only on thing better than a fast big bike, and that's a fa small bike, the Z650 is it.

For motor cycles, small is definitely beautifu If there is one thing that hampers the enjoymen of a bike, it is weight and bulk. The bulkier an heavier a machine the more difficult it is t manouevre, the more trouble it becomes whe cornering and the more fuel it uses.

The Z650 Kawasaki is tangible evidence tha smaller is better. At 495 lb, it weighs some 30 l

...hter than most of the seven fifties and with a ½-in wheelbase is about 3 inches shorter. On the ...ad the bike gives away nothing in performance ...d is far and away a better performer than 550 ... machines. Flat-out mean top speed at MIRA ...as 119·6 mph, only 4 mph down on Suzuki's ...S750 and 2 mph less than the Honda CB750F1.

Even more stunning is its acceleration. Taking the test track like a drag racer, the Z650 ...orched through the quarter-mile in 12·9 sec ...ith a terminal speed of 101·6 mph. Although ...ght runs were timed, six of which were 13 sec or ...der, the bike finished as unruffled as ever.

The secret is not only the power of the twin-...m 652 cc short-stroke, four-cylinder engine, ...t the bike's perfect gearing and balance. The ...650's wheelbase is neither so short as to ...ovoke unmanageable wheelies on take-off nor ...o long that there is too much wheelspin.

Drop the clutch at 7,000 rpm and the Kaw-...saki just digs in and gets on with the job, the ...ont wheel just hovering above the tarmac for ...e first few yards. It is as though the bike was ...ade for drag racing. The proof of this is that the ...650 is one of the quickest bikes from rest ...rough 110 yards. The terminal speed of 66·8 ...ph has only been beaten once – by the super-...st 1973 Kawasaki Z1 903 cc four at 68 mph. It ...n reach 50 mph in just 3 sec from rest.

Yet the bike is no awkward rev-happy racer. ...lthough it can scream up to 10,000 rpm (the red ...ne is at 9,000 rpm), the engine is sweet and ...exible enough to haul along at under 4,000 rpm ...nd there is torque enough to give a sizeable kick ... the seat as you open up.

Apart from a band around 7,000 rpm, the ...650 is exceptionally smooth for a four in-line, ...rticularly at about 70 mph in top gear (equal to 5,500 rpm.) This makes it very relaxing to ride at speed, particularly as there is hardly a hint of 'cammyness' with ample response throughout the range.

Power characteristics like this usually result in above average fuel economy, but although the six-fifty four could return 43·3 mpg around town, the overall test figure of 38·7 mpg was lower than expected, but doubtless due to the heavy consumption of 28·3 mpg during the performance testing. Range on the 4·2 gallon fuel tank is between 150 and 160 miles.

Although Kawasaki claim the machine will run on unleaded fuel like the Z1000, in the case of the test bike unless it was run on premium fuel it would detonate at small throttle openings when pulling hard. This off-idle weakness in the mixture strength was probably connected with the Z650's excessive cold-bloodedness when starting from cold. The process of starting is made more tricky by the need to disengage the clutch when pressing the starter button.

Excellent though the machine is on the track or when ridden hard, the Z650 is not quite so impressive when the going is more relaxed. At low speeds, for example around town streets, the gearchange hangs up and is very clunky, particularly when engaging bottom gear from neutral. On the open road, the gearbox which is identical to the unit on the Z750 twin, is by contrast as slick and crisp as you could want.

Town riding is further spoiled by the excessive backlash in the gearbox, which is compounded by that stuttering in the carburation.

Being much smaller and more compact than the Z1000, the Z650 has none of the bigger model's awe-inspiring bulk, and it is a markedly better handling machine. Although the sus-

pension is softer and more comfortable than the big model one can skim through bends much more confidently than the Z900 or Z1000 would ever allow, and with none of the gut-churning high-speed wobbles that still mark the Z1000 as a bike to be respected when the going gets hot.

The main improvement on the Z650 is a stiffer frame with more sensibly designed steering geometry. The rake of the front fork has been pulled back to 63 degrees, in line with the Z750

twin, and combined with more trail. The bik[e] very stable in fast bends, while at low spe[ed] there is only the slightest hint [of] 'oversteer' – that feeling that the bike want[s to] drop further into a corner – and unlike the Z9[00] it does not want to straighten up when crank[ed] over in fast corners.

Ground clearance is enhanced by use of [a] silencer either side and the only limitation on [the] amount you can crank the bike over is the grip the Dunlop Gold Seal tires. If you manage [to] touch down the left side projection of the ma[in] stand you are a long, long way over.

Harder riders will prefer stiffer springs on [the] Z650, for although it is very much a sport[ing] bike, the suspension has been tailored to hav[e a] broader appeal. The 100 lb/in rear springs giv[e a] smooth ride and the dampers are fairly w[ell] matched – like the front fork.

However, there is still some of the vaguenes[s in] the overall feel of the machine that puts it [not] quite on par with the best handling roadst[er] now available.

Like the GS750 Suzuki, the Z650 has been w[ell] planned for the rider. The seat is soft yet secu[re] enough to prevent you moving about, and t[he] footrests are well tucked in.

The lowish handlebar is properly swept ba[ck] at the right angle and can be adjusted to ta[ste] even though the wiring runs neatly through t[he] tubing. Only general criticism of the Z650 is th[at] the shortness of the bike will put off taller ride[rs.] Cruising at anything over 70 mph becom[es] tiresome after only a few minutes due to t[he] height of the handlebar grips.

Along with practically all other Japanese bik[es] the Z650 has a stainless-steel, front-brake d[isc] which is fine when dry, but always has to [be] allowed for when wet and cold. Kawasa[ki] sensibly resisted the fashionable temptation to [add] another to the rear wheel, and retain a 7-[in] drum brake. This works admirably, the brak[e] being neither too grabby nor under-powere[d.]

Electrical equipment, apart from the hea[d] lamp, is first class. A high power 280-wa[tt] alternator supplies all the needs of the system a[nd]

Specification

Engine: 652 cc (62 × 54 mm) double overhead camshaft, transverse, in-line four. Light-alloy cylinder block and head. Five plain main bearings; plain big ends. Wet sump lubrication; Eaton-type pump. Compression ratio, 9·5 to 1. Four Mikuni 24-mm choke carburettors with lever-operated cold-start jets; paper element air filter. Maximum claimed power, 64 bhp at 8,500 rpm; maximum torque, 42 lb-ft at 7,000 rpm.

Transmission: Primary inverted-tooth chain and spur gears. Wet, multiplate clutch and five-speed gearbox. Overall ratios: 15·6, 10·9, 8·5, 6·96 and 5·95 to 1. Final drive by endless 0·625 × 0·375-in chain. Mph at 1,000 rpm in top gear, 12·8.

Electrical Equipment: Twin coil ignition. 12-volt, 10-amp-hour battery and 280-watt field-excited alternator. 7-in diameter headlamp with 45/40-watt main bulb. Starter motor; four fuses.

Brakes: Hydraulically-operated 11·75-in diameter stainless-steel disc front with single piston floating caliper; 7-in diameter drum rear.

Tires: Dunlop Gold Seal, 3·25 × 19-in F6 ribbed front, 4·00 × 18-in patterned K87 rear.

Suspension: Telescopic front fork. Pivoted rear fork with five-position spring preload adjustment.

Frame: All-welded duplex tube cradle with triple spine tubes.

Dimensions: Wheelbase, 56·5 in; seat height, 32 in; ground clearance, 6·5 in; handlebar width, 29 in; castor angle, 63°; trail, 4·25 in; turning circle, 15 ft 6 in; all unladen.

Weight: 495 lb including one gallon of fuel.

Fuel Capacity: 4·4 gals including reserve.

Sump Oil Capacity: 7·4 pts.

Manufacturer: Kawasaki Heavy Industries (Engine and Motorcycle Group), 1-1 Kawasaki-cho, Akashi-city, Hyogo Pref., Japan.

Performance

Maximum Speeds (Mean): 119·6 mph; 102·7 mph with rider in two-piece oversuit sitting normally.

Best One-way Speed: 121·2 mph – dry track, three-quarter tail wind.

Braking Distance – from 30 mph: 29 ft 3 in.

Fuel Consumption: 38·7 mpg overall.

Oil Consumption: 830 mpp overall.

Minimum Non-snatch Speed: 15 mph in top gear.

Speedo Accuracy:

Indicated mph	30	40	50	60	70	80	90
Actual mph	28·6	37·4	46·2	55·8	63·3	73·8	84·3

Control layout of the Z650 shows the standard Japanese approach with dipswitch, direction indicator switches, horn button and headlamp flasher on the left and light switch, cut out and starter button on the right. Note that the mirrors are too narrow; they should be at least 2 in wider

...nding start tests by grating on the take up and ...bsequently slipping at speed.

...Augmenting the handling well, the brakes are ...bulous, despite the all-up weight of the Lav-...da. Drawback is that the dual discs increase the ...sprung weight over the old drum unit.

...Electrically, the bike was faultless, but we were ...rprised that Laverda have retained the small ...d archaic CEV rear lamp while replacing the ...adlamp with the brilliant Bosch quartz-...logen unit. No praise can be great enough for ...e fabulous air horns. Instruments and switch-...ar are good in quality and convenience.

...Varied and well finished, the toolkit is easily ...und by unscrewing one of the sidepanels, and ...oved sufficient for most of the usual tasks.

...Apart from poorly completed chrome-...rk – nickel was showing through on the ...encers – the general finish of the bike is good. ...e only real snags we feel were a neutral ...mp that flickered on regardlessly towards the ...d of the test, and buckled rear wheel adjuster, ...acy of an attempt to break traction in the ...celeration tests.

...If you are turned on by the Italian looks and ...ra and want a solid and reliable machine – a ...an's bike as they would have said once – then ...e SF is the only machine for you.

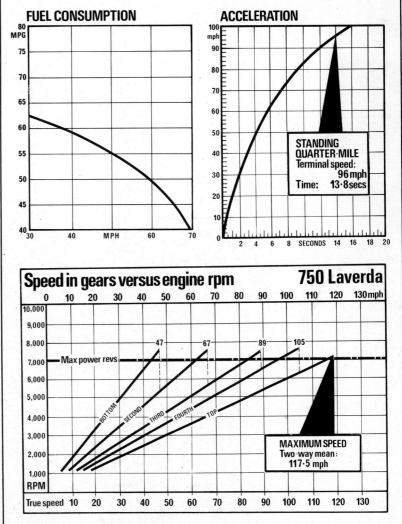

FUEL CONSUMPTION

ACCELERATION

STANDING QUARTER-MILE
Terminal speed: 96 mph
Time: 13·8secs

Speed in gears versus engine rpm **750 Laverda**

Max power revs

47 67 89 105

BOTTOM SECOND THIRD FOURTH TOP

MAXIMUM SPEED
Two-way mean:
117·5 mph

True speed 10 20 30 40 50 60 70 80 90 100 110 120 130

Laverda Jota 1000

Thundering performance is fashionable again, and bikes that can top 135 mph are almost commonplace. But in the mid-1970s the atmosphere was very different. The Middle East oil embargoes had many effects, and one of them was to defuse the power of many of the superbikes. Few had the potential to squeeze past 125 mph and manufacturers had turned to making their products quiet, smooth and comfortable.

An exception was Laverda. Their British importer, Roger Slater, had been campaigning one of their 981 cc three-cylinder models in production racing with great success, and he wanted Laverda to be acclaimed as the fastest machine on sale. The little Italian factory had been making a number of specially tuned models for the British market, the 3CE, and this had proved to be the fastest motor cycle ever tested by *Motor Cycle* at a mean 133·3 mph at MIRA. For continued supremacy in stock racing, particularly the Avon Roadrunner series, some-

thing more potent was necessary, however.

So the Jota was introduced. Like the 3CE, it had a three-cylinder double-overhead camshaft engine, with a novel crank arrangement with the middle piston at top dead centre when the outers were at bottom dead centre, a layout that accentuated the bark of the exhaust even further.

New were five-spoke cast-alloy wheels, disc brakes on both wheels and a neat folding seat with a streamlined tail section. But there were no pretensions to home comforts. The Jota is still a brutal motor cycle, and although it has a larger capacity stablemate in the form of the 1200, it is still one of the fastest you can buy.

The engine is massively powerful and feels it. The unit jangles and rumbles and like a racing engine has a sharply defined power band. When it hits the band the exhaust crackles and the bike catapults the rider forward breathtakingly. Not for nothing are the handlebars adjustable into a racing position – you need it to stay on.

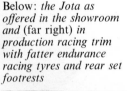

Below: *the Jota as offered in the showroom and* (far right) *in production racing trim with fatter endurance racing tyres and rear set footrests*

At the test track the Jota (Italian for a quick ance for three, so they say) proved its supremacy by topping the 3CE by over 4 mph. Its mean two-way top speed was 137·8 mph – miles faster than anything else then currently available and it was the first over-the-counter production roadster to better 140 mph in one direction with a figure of 140·04 mph.

In racing the Jota was fully justified after winning the Avon series in the hands of Peter Davies in 1976.

For racing some degree of compromise is necessary so there are a number of options available. The air filter can be dispensed with, as we did, the exhaust system offers less resistance than normal (to the level of being illegal in many European countries) and the gearbox can have very close ratios (which were fitted to the test bike, the one raced by Davies). A change in the layshaft return gear closes up the gaps between the gears. Bottom gear, at 9·5 to 1, is 18 percent higher than the standard ratio.

With or without the options, the Jota makes a fabulous machine. On the road, steering and roadholding are both beyond reproach while the braking is simply eye-popping. The engine has a lazy sounding note that makes the acceleration extremely deceptive. Open up the three Delorto carbs and the rest of the world seems to go into reverse.

With the close-ratio gearbox and highest gearing the speeds at maximum revs in each cog read like science fiction. Normally, the Laverda 3C revs to 7,500 rpm, as marked on the Japanese-made Nippon Denso rev counter, but the Jota can be revved safely to 8,500, though 8,000 is more than enough. At eight, the high bottom gear goes on forever, peaking out at 64 mph, second takes you on to 88 mph, third whistles past the ton to 111 mph, fourth is good enough to beat any 1976 machine in top at 130 mph and top gear peaks at 141 mph.

Not surprisingly, riding the Jota in town is made more awkward as the practical minimum speed in bottom gear is a shade over 10 mph, and some clutch slipping is needed when pulling away quickly from rest.

This showed up convincingly during the standing quarter mile tests. It was impossible to use full power when slipping the clutch for fear of frying the plates and the sticky Dunlop endurance tyre fitted prevented spinning the rear wheel. So the first few yards of the quarter-mile were taken gingerly and chopped vital seconds from the elapsed time.

Despite this, the Jota thundered down the strip to record a mean time of 13·05 sec with a terminal speed of 110·55 mph. Geared for the quarter, there is no doubt that the bike would have clocked very low twelves at around 113 mph.

Either way, the Jota can blow off anything on the road.

What is remarkable about the Jota is that this performance is achieved without sacrificing too many of the manners expected of a roadster. The bike produces a magnificent sound – winding open the throttle at low revs releases a sharp bark from the three-into-two exhaust system that mellows into a crisp wail on full power. But the engine runs happily on premium fuel despite the 10 to 1 compression ratio and, being so big, has adequate torque for quick getaways in almost any circumstances.

All the same, there is always the animal in the bike lurking in the depths of its massive crankcase. It whirrs and whines, particularly the triplex primary chain and never really likes being run at less than a fast lick.

The reason lies in the power characteristics. The double-overhead-camshaft head contains racing cams which are only happy in opening the bucket-follower operated valves at over 5,000 rpm, preferably with the aid of a megaphone exhaust. This gives 90 bhp at 7,600 rpm.

The effect is most distinctive in top gear. Below 70 mph the engine baulks at full throttle. But at 90 it becomes interested, at the ton it is on the boil and beyond that the bike feels like it will keep accelerating for ever.

accommodate a broad variety of rider statur

The controls blend beautifully to the ride hands. Both levers are contoured and the finge slide over them naturally. The switches, identic almost to those found on Suzukis, are su stantial, neat and very easy to use.

Apart from a heavy clutch action and a ge change which could occasionally be noisy in t lower gears, the controls generally set a very hi standard. So the rider is in a good position sample the Laverda's excellent handling to t full.

The steering, which has unusual geomet resulting from fork legs which are parallel to t steering stem, is natural at all speeds and the bi can be cranked over without need for correctic at the handlebar to hold a line.

Only criticism is a slight jumpiness in t steering that occurs above 90 mph which is cure as when the bike is raced by Slater, by using t racing yokes from the 750 SFC production race bringing the forks parallel to the stem.

The cornering clearance is immense, to despite the large generator cover, and in road u the rider need have no fear of touching an thing. Even so, Roger Slater feels he has to stiffe up the suspension which, in day-to-day circun stances, is a perfect compromise between ric

Specification

Engine: 981 cc (75 × 74 mm) double-overhead camshaft, transverse, in-line three. Light-alloy cylinder block and head. Four caged-roller main bearings with needle roller outrigger on drive side; caged-roller big ends. Wet sump lubrication with gear pump and oil cooler. Compression ratio, 10 to 1. Three 32-mm choke Delorto carburettors with lever-operated cold-start jets; optional paper element air filter. Maximum claimed power, 90 bhp at 7,600 rpm.

Transmission: Triplex primary chain with slipper tensioner. Wet, multiplate clutch and five-speed gearbox. Overall ratios: 9·51, 6·90, 5·45, 4·65 and 4·29 to 1. Final drive by 0·625 × 0·375-in chain with vane type shock absorber in rear-wheel hub. Mph at 1,000 rpm in top gear, 17·7.

Electrical Equipment: Bosch electronic flywheel-magneto ignition with external coils. 12-volt, 27-amp-hour battery and 125-watt alternator. 7·5-in diameter headlamp with 60/55-watt halogen main bulb. Starter motor and four fuses.

Brakes: Hydraulically-operated Brembo 11-in (279-mm) diameter double disc front, single rear with double-acting calipers.

Tires: Dunlop TT100, 4·10 × S18-in front, 4·25 × S18-in rear. Cast light-alloy wheels.

Suspension: Ceriani telescopic front fork. Pivoted rear fork with Ceriani spring damper units and three-position spring preload adjustment.

Frame: Welded duplex cradle with 2·5-in diameter spine.

Dimensions: Wheelbase, 58·5 in; ground clearance, 5·5 in; seat height, 32·5 in; castor angle 63°; trail, 5·5 in; turning circle 16 ft; all unladen.

Weight: 522 lb including approximately one gallon of fuel.

Fuel Capacity: 5·1 gals including 3·6 pts reserve.

Sump Oil Capacity: 5·5 pt.

Manufacturer: Moto Laverda SpA, 36042 Breganze, Italy.

Performance

Maximum Speeds (Mean): 137·8 mph; 125·95 mph with rider in two-piece outfit sitting normally.

Best One-way Speed: 140·04 mph – dry track, slight tail wind.

Braking Distance – from 30 mph: 25 ft 5 in.

Fuel Consumption: 35·4 mpg overall.

Oil Consumption: approximately 420 mpp overall.

Minimum Non-snatch Speed: 24 mph in top gear.

Speedo Accuracy:

Indicated mph	30	40	50	60	70	80	90
Actual mph	28·9	38·4	47·9	58·9	69·9	80·9	91·9

Nevertheless, it can still run economically, returning 35·4 mpg, giving well over 150 miles range on the 4·8 gallon tank.

As well as offering stunning performance, Laverda make the Jota more appealing by not losing sight of the need for a quality of finish and detailing that puts other Italian bikes to shame.

On the Jota there is a cosy seat that hinges up and is lockable, superb instruments which are also very accurate and – something of a rarity on any bike – fully adjustable hand and foot controls.

The handlebar can be raised from a full racing position to a normal touring stance in minutes with socket key while the footrests can be rotated, giving almost 3 inches of adjustment. Variable length gear levers are also available. The upshot is that although the seat is fairly high at 32 inches, the slim profile of the bike can

nd road holding but which squats too much nder the immense cornering loads offered by the unlop tires and limits clearance on the right.

Compared with the 3CE, a larger section 4·25- rear tire is used on the Jota, which is made ore secure by using a negative angle on the face f the cast light-alloy wheel to hold the tire bead gainst the side walls of the rim. The idea is to get tter traction at the back end, but if you are like eter Davies and prefer a little more, fit the unlop Endurance KR91 tires as were used at e Hutchinson 100 races when Peter came cond and were still fitted when we tested the ike at MIRA. The grip with these is massive but, evertheless, they still had shortcomings. Power- g out of the 90 mph bends on the MIRA No. 2 rcuit resulted in some wiggles at the back end, ut you had to be right on the limit to provoke it.

With three 11-in discs, the braking was as good s can be on a machine weighing 504 lb. The tires elped particularly to give a 30 mph stopping istance of 25 ft.

A chain drive the Jota may have, but it is ngineered for the minimum of problems by orrect geometry relative to the swinging arm ivot (incidentally now on needle bearings) and hain wear is very low.

Everything else is just as one should expect of a machine of its price bracket. Lighting from the 60-watt halogen headlamp is more than ade- quate for the bike's speed, the tools are generous and strong while the finish is 100 per cent.

The electric starting may be noisy but it is reliable. Further impressive features are the easy- to-use main stand, fuss-free electronic ignition and a pair of horns that would wake the dead (let alone car drivers!). Altogether, the barrel- chested Jota is a rider's bike, the sort of machine that responds best to skilful and attentive riding.

Handlebars on Laverdas are fully adjustable

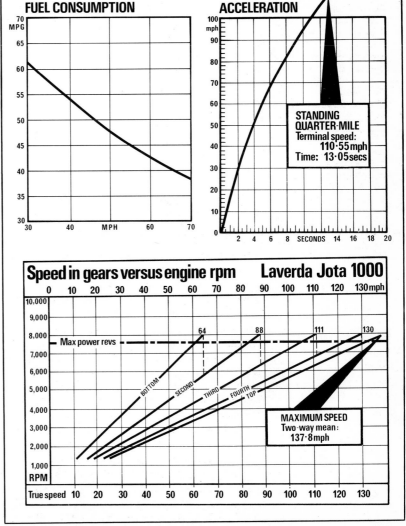

FUEL CONSUMPTION

ACCELERATION

STANDING QUARTER-MILE
Terminal speed: 110·55 mph
Time: 13·05 secs

Speed in gears versus engine rpm — Laverda Jota 1000

Max power revs

64   88   111   130

BOTTOM SECOND THIRD FOURTH TOP

MAXIMUM SPEED
Two-way mean: 137·8 mph

Moto Guzzi Le Mans 850

No Compromise! That clarion call would probably be denied by many of the Italian factories like Moto Guzzi, but it is obvious from their undiluted sporting machines that they will go to any lengths to satisfy that aim.

The 844 cc Le Mans is a classic case. Offered by Moto Guzzi as the top of the range sportster in 1976 it was neither fast for its size or particularly quick over the quarter mile compared to many other outwardly less potent machines. But where it counts, on the open road or on the race tracks, the mighty Le Mans has few peers. It is both fast and agile and responds well to tuning, as has been borne out by the marque's overwhelming success in production machine racing.

Like Ducati, Moto Guzzi have paid close attention to the basic credentials of the machine.

Basic hardwear for the production road racer or the high-speed cruiser alike; the 850 cc Moto Guzzi Le Mans vee-twin

As the name of the bike suggests it is close associated with racing. Le Mans is the home the 24-hour Bol d'Or endurance race and whi not having the same level of success as Ducati this type of competition, Moto Guzzi learned th same lessons: that a slim and light motor cyc with a very stiff frame can afford to give awa disproportionate amounts of horsepower t more unweildy but potent racers.

It is ironic that the engine of the Le Mans wa never originally intended for a motor cycl Developed as a lightweight power unit for military cross country vehicle it did howeve have obvious potential for a two-wheeler. Bein a 90-degree vee-twin it has the inherent smooth ness and rhythm that has always been appealin to motor cyclists.

The first engines, with a 700 cc capacity, were [pu]t into touring bikes, placed across the frame so [tha]t it was natural that the transmission should [ha]ve shaft drive. This has remained on the Le [M]ans, proving a boon in long-distance racing.

The engine is ideal for a motor cycle for one [ba]sic reason. Not only is it smooth, but its [nar]row crankcase means that it can be set low [do]wn in the frame for light handling and still give [a l]arge degree of ground clearance.

The unit is extremely robustly built. External [ri]bing on the cases and a massive forged single-[thr]ow crankshaft are further strengthened by [num]erous plain main and big-end bearings. There [ar]e many similarities to the BMW, but a very [sig]nificant difference is that the camshaft is above [th]e crankshaft, in the crotch of the vee with short [pu]shrods and rockers opening the valves. With [lig]hter valve gear, the Guzzi is far less sensitive to [ov]er-revving than the BMW.

[B]ore and stroke are slightly oversquare, at 83 [m]m by 78 mm, and the barrels are interesting for [th]eir chrome plated bores which are unique on a [fo]ur-stroke motor cycle.

And as befits a sports machine, the level of [tu]ne is comparable to the early works endurance [ra]cers. Compression ratio is a hefty 10·2 to 1 and [th]e engine breaths through two 36-mm choke [De]lorto carburettors with no more filtering than [a c]ouple of velocity stacks and stone guards.

Yet apart from a level of bustling noise that is [no]t totally out of place on the bike, there is an [ini]tial indication of the Le Mans' civility. It starts [up] from cold promptly after using the starting jet [lev]er and punching the electric starter button on

the right-hand clip-on handlebar. And it runs cleanly on premium fuel despite the high compression ratio – this hints at good combustion chamber design. The feeling of utter civility ends when you open up the Le Mans. The loud gasping from the intakes indicates that the bike wants to go fast. Unlike the touring 850-T3 model, the Le Mans develops comparatively little torque at low revs and wills the rider to go faster and faster.

The bike has a pleasant long-legged feel too that makes it deceptively fast despite the over-optimism of the speedometer.

Specification

Engine: 844 cc (83 × 78 mm) overhead valve, transverse, 90° vee-twin. Light-alloy heads and barrels; chrome-plated bores. Two plain main bearings; plain big ends. Wet sump lubrication; gear pump. Compression ratio, 10·2 to 1. Two Delorto PHF 36-mm choke carburettors with accelerator pumps; cable-operated cold-start jets. Claimed maximum power, 80 bhp at 7,300 rpm.

Transmission: Two-plate dry clutch on crankshaft to primary spur gears (ratio 21/17). Five-speed gearbox. Overall ratios: 11·64, 8·08, 6·1, 5·06 and 4·37 to 1. Final drive by shaft and spiral-bevel gears (ratio 33/7). Mph at 1,000 rpm in top gear, 16·7.

Electrical Equipment: Coil ignition. 12-volt, 32-amp-hour battery and 280-watt alternator. 7-in diameter headlamp with 45/40-watt main bulb. Four fuses with spares. Starter motor.

Brakes: Brembo hydraulically-operated 11·75-in diameter perforated cast-iron double disc front, 9·5-in diameter rear. Front left and rear controlled by foot pedal with load limiting on rear.

Tires: Metzeler, 3·25 × V18-in front ribbed. Avon Roadrunner, 4·10 × V18-in rear. Cast aluminium-alloy wheels.

Suspension: Moto Guzzi telescopic front fork. Pivoted rear fork with five-position spring preload adjustment.

Frame: Welded duplex tube cradle with removable bottom tubes.

Dimensions: Wheelbase, 59 in; ground clearance, 7·5 in; seat height, 29·5 in; handlebar width, 29 in; castor angle 61°; trail, 3·8 in; turning circle, 15 ft 3 in; all unladen.

Weight: 485 lb including approximately one gallon of fuel.

Fuel Capacity: 6 gals including 6 pts reserve.

Sump Oil Capacity: 5 pt.

Manufacturer: Siemm Moto Guzzi SpA, Mandello del Lario, Como, Italy.

Performance

Maximum Speeds (Mean): 123·4 mph; 115 mph with rider sitting normally.
Best One-way Speed: 125·9 mph – dry track, 10 mph three-quarter tail wind.
Braking Distance – from 30 mph: 30 ft 4 in.
Fuel Consumption: 33 mpg.
Oil Consumption: 312 mpp overall.
Minimum Non-snatch Speed: 16 mph in top gear.
Speedo Accuracy:

Indicated mph	30	40	50	60	70	80	90
Actual mph	21·6	30·4	39·2	47·8	56·4	66·5	76·6

High-speed cruising at an indicated 125 to 1 mph could be comfortably indulged in. The fa that this is a true speed of around 110 mph mal it no less impressive, particularly as the Le Ma is totally secure and smooth at this speed.

With the rider flat on the tank the mean t speed at MIRA was 123·4 mph at 7,500 rpm top gear. With the engine developing a claim 80 bhp at 7,300 rpm this suggests that the Mans is perfectly geared for its power outp The riding position is more of a racing crou with the clip-on handlebars and rear-mount footrests urging the rider to keep out of t breeze behind the small fairing. Like this the Mans can still clock 115 mph, making it one the fastest roadsters, even in 1978 when t quicker seven-fifties can top 125 mph flat out b are less flexible and unsuitable for continuo high-speed riding due to their sit-up-and-b riding stances.

With a top gear ratio of 4·37 to 1 and t loping beat of the engine, the Le Mans pleasing lacks the busy nature of the Japanese fours. B the overall high gearing, and the closeness of t five gearbox ratios, which are part of the reas for the bike's suitability for racing, spoil t standing quarter mile potential.

Figures of 14 sec and 98·9 mph are hard impressive, equating only with touring bik (indeed, this is only 0·1 sec slower than the 85 T3). A closer look at the acceleration gra shows that a full second is lost on the initial sta which with the additional 4 mph at the end of t run translates into a respectable figure.

Why this is so is not difficult to see. Botto gear is fairly high and although the two-plate d clutch is light in action it does not like taking the drive on full blooded starts. The shaft dri also makes life difficult by extending the re suspension and limiting the amount of whe spin possible.

By far the most impressive feature of t machine is its handling. Made of straight thic walled tubing the frame is immensely strong a at high speed the bike has a degree of securi that is uncanny. Like the feel of the engine, it h the effect of giving the impression that t machine is going much slower than it really i

The suspension and front fork are w balanced, with optimum spring rates and dam ing, the only fault being the difficulty of alteri the rear spring preload adjusters which a obscured by the close proximity of the silence.

Like all in-line machines there is some torq reaction from the crankshaft when blipping t throttle or when changing gear quickly. It c also be embarrassing when you miss a gea which is quite easy on the Le Mans because of t inordinate length of the lever and the need change gear slowly to prevent clunks.

The steering is superb. Complimenting t high speed handling with tautness, the fork, wi a 61 degree rake angle and 3·8 inches of tra gives a totally different feel from a Ducati with lightness at low speed that makes dense traffic good deal less daunting.

The brakes are equally brilliant. Unique on a current two-wheeler the brakes offer feel and immense power arising from the use of the connected rear and front left discs. These are operated from the foot lever and for normal use nothing else is needed. But for real eye-popping stops the other hand lever-operated front disc can be called into action. Being nearly of 12-in diameter in perforated cast iron, the discs can lock the wheel at the will of the rider.

But for balanced use the rear disc is only 9 in and is more than good enough. The only limitation on braking is the quality and condition of the tires.

The basic electrical gear on the Le Mans should be a model for other manufacturers too. A massive 280-watt alternator sits on the front of the crankshaft and feeds a monster 32-amp-hour battery. But the headlamp is a 45-watt unit that could usefully be replaced by a quartz-halogen unit, and the switchgear is the Mickey-Mouse-like barrel type first seen on Benellis that is neither reliable or easy to use.

So under the skin of the Le Mans is a motor cycle of indisputable quality. The surface lets it down, for the finish is very poor. The seat, a single moulding in foam rubber split soon after the bike was picked up; this was changed in design during late 1977 – it may be an improvement. The lining on the tank soon peeled after fuel was spilled on it and the matt of the exhaust pipes was soon tarnished.

This bike has plenty to offer the competitive sporting rider. If he is able to overlook the wrinkles then the road rider too should be rewarded by the basic integrity of the Guzzi Le Mans.

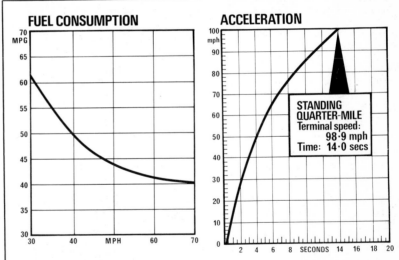

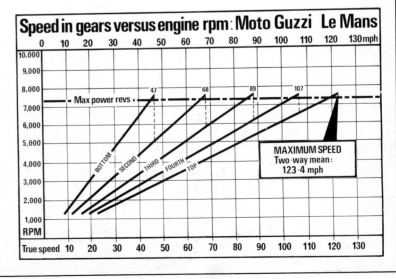

MV Agusta 750S America

A motor cycle is more than a means of getting from A to B and can offer even more than the fun and freedom with which it is popularly associated. A motor cycle can be a passport to a fantasy existence. And the most convincing proof of this is the MV Agusta 750S America.

A dream in its red finish, set off by matt silver castings and gold alloy wheels, the 750S is more than a motor cycle. Riding one transports you into the fantasy worlds of the works racer and the millionaire – both at once. The mixture of a racing riding stance with low-mounted instruments and controls, the slim and sonorous four-

cylinder engine and the roar of the exhaust impossible to match on two wheels anywhere

But dreaming apart, even in these days wh four-cylinder sports bikes are commonplace, MV has plenty to offer, despite a price tag t can be very high when all the standard extras optioned for.

With these, which include a fairing, rear d brake and magnesium-alloy cast wheels, and 812 cc engine conversion that boosts power around 100 bhp for a top speed of 140 mph, price goes even higher!

Designed originally for the United Sta

rket – as the name suggests – the 750S Amer-
is also the biggest MV ever sold. Standard
pacity is 790 cc enabling MV to provide extra
xibility over the previous 750 cc models.

As it was aimed strictly at the USA market, the
merica offers a degree of civility and manners
seen on an MV before. Not only does the big
r provide scintillating performance and
ndling but also it does so now with more
mfort, less sound (although what is still there is
t as spine chilling as ever), and without
ssibility of sucking dirt that the old seven-
ies were able to do. The 750S America has an
filter, one that would not look out of place on
mass-produced Japanese multi.

Tested by *Motor Cycle* at MIRA, the big MV
corded a top speed of 120 mph, an achievement
t would have been bettered by some 10 mph
d the 1,500-yd confines of the timing strip not
nspired against the machine's high gearing. As
was, the 750S was still accelerating in top gear
it passed through the timing lights.

In the 812 cc 850 Monza form, achieved by
ring out the cylinders, fitting hairier camshafts
d bigger pistons and dispensing with the air
er and restrictive silencers, the MV was much
ster.

On the timing strip it clocked a mean 130 mph,
t with a longer run in on the mile-long
aights at MIRA achieved 144 mph in one
rection with the rider flat on the tank for a

*The MV Agusta 750S
America can be obtained
in standard trim* (left), *or
with all the extras* (far
left), *that include
magnesium alloy wheels,
a disc rear brake and a
full fairing. Further
options can boost engine
power to over 100 bhp
and top speed to
140 mph*

Specification

Engine: 790 cc (67 × 56 mm) double-overhead camshaft, transverse, in-line four. Light-alloy cylinder head and barrels; cast-iron liners. Six roller main bearings; needle roller big ends. Wet sump lubrication; gear pump. Compression ratio, 9·5 to 1. Four 26-mm choke VHB Delorto carburettors with lever-operated cold-start jets; foam element air filter. Maximum claimed power, 75 bhp at 8,500 rpm. Maximum torque, 48 lb-ft at 7,500 rpm.

Transmission: Primary helical gears. Wet, multiplate clutch and five-speed gearbox. Overall ratios: 11·84, 8·4, 6·37, 5·52 and 4·97 to 1. Final drive by bevel gears and shaft. Mph at 1,000 rpm in top gear, 15·2.

Electrical Equipment: Coil and distributor ignition. 12-volt, 32-amp-hour battery and belt-driven 135-watt dc dynamo-starter. 7-in diameter headlamp with 60/55-watt halogen main bulb. Four fuses; direction indicators.

Brakes: Scarab 11-in diameter double disc front, 10-in diameter rear.

Tires: Metzeler, 3·50 × 18-in ribbed front, 4·00 × 18-in C7 block rear. Cast magnesium-alloy wheels.

Suspension: Ceriani telescopic front fork. Pivoted rear fork with manual five-position spring preload adjustment.

Frame: Duplex tube cradle frame.

Dimensions: Wheelbase, 55 in; seat height, 30 in; ground clearance, 7 in; handlebar width, 28 in; castor angle, 63°; trail, 3·2 in; turning circle, 17 ft 9 in; all unladen.

Weight: 510 lb including one gallon of fuel.

Fuel Capacity: 5 gals including 8·4 pts reserve.

Sump Oil Capacity: 7·9 pts.

Manufacturer: Meccanica Verghera SpA, viale Adriatico 50, 21010 Verghera (Varese).

Performance

Maximum Speeds (Mean): 120·2 mph; 115·7 mph with rider sitting normally.
Best One-way Speed: 122·1 mph – dry track, slight tail wind.
Braking Distance – from 30 mph: 28 ft 9 in.
Fuel Consumption: 38·4 mpg.
Oil Consumption: 625 mpp.
Minimum Non-snatch Speed: 23 mph in top gear.
Speedo Accuracy:

Indicated mph	30	40	50	60	70	80	90
Actual mph	29·6	38·6	47·7	57·4	67·2	77·7	88·6

mean two-way figure of 140 mph.

On the road there is no denying the MV heritage. Crouched down behind the fairing t sensations are just the same as being on a rac

The screen is wrapped tightly around the no of the bike without a millimetre to spare and t engine below you produces all the busy racket a unit built with dozens of ball and roll bearings to run with minimum friction.

Snap the throttles in neutral and the mot reacts with an immediate, momentous whoo Do it with 6,000 already showing on the r counter in top gear and it thrusts you forwa with contemptuous ease.

The four slides on the 26-mm choke VH Delorto carbs are controlled by a single cab and, like all the controls, operate with maximu co-operation for the rider.

The MV is a machine that makes no excus for itself. And finished in bright red with a blac suede seat that can accommodate two by movi the rear section back 3 inches, it lacks nothin but subtlety.

Based on the 500 cc four-cylinder racir design of the 1950s and 1960s, the doubl overhead camshaft engine could never be ma produced. Beautifully cast in satin finished allo the crankcases are a one-piece casting into whic the crankshaft assembly, separate cylind barrels and one-piece head are bolted. Eve shaft is supported in either roller or ball bearin and the cams are driven by a train of gea between the centre cylinders.

One of the pleasures of running the MV starting it up in the morning and identifying a the variety of sounds coming from it.

The starting and generating system is uniqu To keep the engine slim (it is as narrow as mo twins) the combined starter-generator is driv by a pair of belts beneath the gearbox. With massive 32-amp-hour battery to power th starter, it never baulked even in frosty weathe But the engine is naturally cold blooded and too several miles to warm up.

Only real concession to road use in th transmission is the shaft final drive. Otherwis the five-speed gearbox is pure competition styl the gearchange losing nothing in being switche to the left-hand side and snicking through th ratios with the precision of a camera shutter.

The only dubious aspect of the drive train i the clutch. For although it was impressivly ligh in action and smooth in taking up the drive, i swelled badly after being slipped when getting o the mark in acceleration tests. Nevertheless, wit a bottom gear giving 58 mph at 9,000 rpm, ther was sufficient power to lift the front wheel an push the bike to 60 mph in under 5 sec!

Over 30 mph the MV handles very well. At lo speeds the weight and riding position give a sligh unwieldy feeling, but the opposite is true once th machine is given its head. The steering tautens improving with speed and the bike become utterly secure. Between 80 mph and 100 mph th MV is rock steady and the combination of very responsive engine, minimal vibration,

The MV Agusta four-cylinder engine is very slim from the use of a dynamo beneath the gearbox and an ignition distributor behind the cylinders

...perb high speed riding position and one of the ...eatest sounds in motor cycling is an experience ...fficult to beat.

It is not the sort of bike you could recommend ...r long distance riding though. The Ceriani ...spension is very hard and while offering good ...ntrol for a bike of the MV's weight gives a ...ugh ride over anything but the smoothest of ...rfaces. High speed cornering is secure but the ...ound clearance wanting, as the side and main ...ands touch down very easily. With two discs on ...e front wheel and one on the rear, the braking ...a model of perfection. Made by either Scarab ...Brembo, the discs are in cast iron with light-...loy double-acting calipers. At any speed, the ...ightest touch of the hand lever or foot pedal ...ves instant action without fear of locking the ...heels. The brakes work very well in the wet too.

In its 790 cc form, the MV is fairly economical ...run, giving an average 38·4 mpg which with ...e 5 gallon fuel tank gives a reasonable range of ...0 miles, a distance greater than can be ...mfortably managed anyway because of the ...rd springing. However, with hard use, the ...nsumption can drop to 29 mpg and in the 812 ...form this can go as low as 25 mpg. In either ...rm, high octane fuel is imperative.

The MV Agusta 750S America and the 850 ...onza are bikes for the committed and wealthy ...nnoisseur. Many Japanese machines can ...ovide similar specifications and even have ...tter performance, but none can compare to the ...V's quality of sight and sound. The MV is to be ...dden *and* experienced. And with the America ...ving thrown off its previous reputation for ...ving poor detailing and finish, it has risen to ...ing one of the true classic motor cycles.

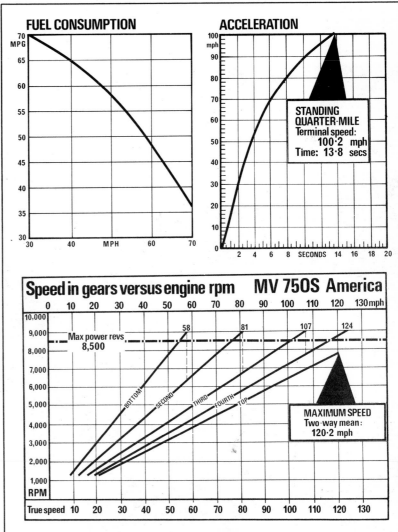

FUEL CONSUMPTION

ACCELERATION

STANDING QUARTER-MILE
Terminal speed: 100·2 mph
Time: 13·8 secs

Speed in gears versus engine rpm **MV 750S America**

Max power revs 8,500

MAXIMUM SPEED
Two-way mean: 120·2 mph

Norton Commando 850 Mk 3

Irony always accompanied the Norton Commando. Introduced in the late 1960s as a smooth and refined version of the traditional big British twin, its essential character was one dear to the heart of the enthusiast fond of the basic values in motor cycles. It was fast, lusty, lithe and light and virtues such as easy starting and quietness didn't fit into the conception.

The early 750 cc models were quick, with top speeds close to 120 mph and a combination of blinding acceleration and flexibility that has rarely been matched. Then the 828 cc models which were introduced in 1973 in an effort to improve reliability proved even better. They were tough, handled well and using Norton's patented rubber mountings for the engine and trans-

mission were very smooth at high speed.

But the tough American noise regulations a: a desire to appeal to a wider market spelled t end for the performance image. Three years lat the final form of the Commando, the Mark appeared with electric starting, better comfo disc brakes on both wheels and barely a whisp from the exhaust.

The irony was that when the Comman finally competed successfully against the Japa ese competition in refinement, financial pro lems at the manufacturers, Norton-Villie Triumph, led to the end of its production favour of the Triumph Trident, which w regarded as a more modern machine. The la Commando Mark 3 eight-fifties were complet

early 1977 while the Marston Road, Wolverampton, factory was in the hands of the Official Receiver. The penalty that was paid for the civilized nature of those last Nortons was in acceleration. While the early Commandos weighed around 440 lb, the last Mark 3 versions tipped the scales at over 500 lb, enough to add a second to the standing quarter-mile times. With a time of 14·4 sec and a terminal speed of 90 mph it was little better than most 550 cc machines of the day.

The appeal of the Commando lay in its instant engine response. The layout of the engine and transmission with the 828 cc long-stroke parallel twin and separate four-speed gearbox was straight from the 1950s. Major differences were that the triplex chain primary drive had in the final form a tensioner and, as on the original Commandos, an all-metal diaphragm spring clutch.

The engine itself, with a bore and stroke of 77 mm by 89 mm, has a crankshaft with two roller main bearings and with a compression ratio of 8 to 1 was in a very soft state of tune. Developing 52 bhp at 6,000 rpm, it was as unobtrusive as an engine could be yet packed a punch from low revs that made the gearbox almost unnecessary.

The bike was still able to cruise comfortably and smoothly at 90 mph, but much of the old liveliness had been lost. Unlike the older eight-fifties, which would rev safely to over 7,000 rpm, the Mark 3 is at its best between 2,000 and 4,000 rpm. It pulls hard from 1,500 but beyond 6,000 the restrictive air intake and exhaust silencing cuts the power drastically. And there is no point at all in revving to 6,500 rpm.

Normally, such a lazy and relaxing type of power delivery makes a bike easy and undemanding to ride, and this is true up to a point on the Mark 3.

The four-speed gearbox complements the engine well and the drive is delightfully smooth, the rubber vane dampers in the rear wheel, added to ease the load on the gearbox, giving a snatch-free ride at no more than a walking pace in bottom gear. But the overall gearing is very high with a top gear ratio of 4·18 to 1. This, the optimum gearing for the engine, giving 6,000 rpm when the rider is flat on the tank at the top speed of 115 mph. At 70 mph, the unit is ticking over at a modest 3,800 rpm. The motor never feels that it is working hard, and there is never anything that could be called vibration at motorway cruising speeds.

However, the characteristics of the rubber engine mounting system made slow riding a chore. While the rubber units absorb the vibration at normal engine revs, an inescapable feature of the system is that it resonates at certain rev bands. On the Commando this is at 2,000 rpm. With the high gearing this occurs at 40 mph in top gear (a perfectly feasible speed for the torquey engine). The rider has to keep changing gear just to avoid the resonant vibrations. Fortunately the gear change is very good. None could be more creamy or positive in action, even though the lever has been transferred to the left-hand side of the bike.

In their day Norton Commandos were unbeatable in production machine racing and even in its final form the Mark III 850 cc twin exhibited the same legendary handling

Another poor aspect of town riding was a result of weak carburation, most obvious in throttle response where it showed as an occasional spit back through the two 30-mm choke Amal Concentric carburettors. The idling mixture control was near perfect, giving an excellent 500 rpm idling speed even after a brisk run; a period of slow running in town heated up the carbs enough to cause stalling. This was not the

headache in traffic that it used to be – just touch of the green twistgrip-mouthed button a the electric starter spins the engine back into li

It is not always like that – from cold, the Am carbs still need messy flooding and the star motor occasionally baulks at turning the engi over against compression without moment from the crank's massive flywheel. And althou we are assured of its normality, the crunching the backfire-overload device when the engi stops sounds horrible. Such things are eas forgotten once you take the Commando for cross-country spin. For like the Triumph T dent, the Norton Commando's handling is ju great. The steering is neutral throughout t speed range and flicking into a bend needs more than a nudge. Moreover, the bike fee absolutely secure when cranked over with t footrests lightly skimming the tarmac.

The other side of the coin is the poor ri quality of the stiff suspension. Small ripples a transmitted undiminished to the rider's han and once caused the front wheel to step out in bend. Only the bigger bumps are absorbed.

In this the Commando is no better and worse than most contemporary bikes, althou the deeper seat Norton use to absorb the bum in fact spoils the comfort of the machine.

Without moving back the footrests to suit t long tank of the Interstate version (the te model), too much weight is placed on the rider behind at speed and he wallows around on t padding. The seat cover is too thin, too, ar under full acceleration the seat pan slipped ar ripped through the material at the front.

Commando braking can be very good, e pecially now with the disc rear brake. The fro brake lever is neatly curved to fit the hand an the power is immense. The rear unit was spoilt t an out-of-true disc and a leaking master cylinde

Likewise the electrics of the bike are good wit an exceptionally powerful 60-watt H4 quartz

Specification

Engine: 828 cc (77 × 89 mm) overhead valve, parallel twin. Light-alloy head. Two caged-roller main bearings; plain big ends. Dry sump lubrication. Compression ratio, 8·5 to 1. Two 32-mm Amal carburettors with handlebar lever operated cold-start slides; washable oil-soaked air filter. Claimed maximum power, 58 bhp at 5,900 rpm.
Transmission: Triplex primary chain. Wet, multiplate clutch with diaphragm spring and four-speed gearbox. Overall ratios: 10·71, 6·84, 5·1 and 4·18 to 1. Final drive by 0·625 × 0·375-in chain. Mph at 1,000 rpm in top gear, 20.
Electrical Equipment: Twin coil ignition with ballast resistor. 12-volt, 13-amp-hour battery and 120-watt alternator with twin Zener diode charge control. 7-in diameter headlamp with 60/55-watt halogen main bulb. Starter motor, direction indicators, headlamp flasher, accessory terminal.
Brakes: Hydraulically-operated 10·7-in diameter disc front and rear.
Tires: Dunlop K81, 4·10 × 19 in front and rear.
Suspension: Telescopic front fork. Pivoted rear fork with three-position spring preload adjustment. Girling dampers.
Frame: Duplex tube frame with 2-in spine and rubber suspension for engine-transmission unit.
Dimensions: Wheelbase, 57 in; seat height, 32 in; ground clearance, 6 in; overall length, 88 in; turning circle, 18 ft 6 in; all unladen.
Weight: 486 lb with one gallon of fuel.
Fuel Capacity: 6·25 gals including about 7 pts reserve.
Oil Tank Capacity: 6·3 pts.
Manufacturer: Norton Villiers Ltd, Marston Road, Wolverhampton.

Performance

Maximum Speeds (Mean): 114·9 mph; 96·9 mph with rider in two-piece outfit sitting normally.
Best One-way Speed: 115·4 mph – dry track, slight cross wind.
Braking Distance – from 30 mph: 28 ft.
Fuel Consumption: 36 mpg overall.
Oil Consumption: 580 mpp overall.
Minimum Non-snatch Speed: 16 mph in top gear.
Speedo Accuracy:

Indicated mph	30	40	50	60	70	80	90	100
Actual mph	30·3	40·6	50·9	61·2	71·5	82·5	93·4	104·3

Besides being dated with its long-stroke pushrod engine and separate gearbox, the performance of the Commando was spoilt by restrictive silencing and the extra weight of equipment like electric starting to satisfy the American market

alogen headlamp offering a sharp pencil main eam and a well cut-off dip. The switchgear and ontrols are equal to anything on a Japanese achine. The clutch lever pull is light and nooth while all the necessary switches are in sy reach.

Maintenance has been eased on the latest 50, too, the most significant modification eing the use of easily adjustable rubber ngine/transmission mountings. Since the rear-heel fork was mounted to the rear of the earbox plates, excessive side play affected the andling adversely. This used to be adjusted for de clearance with steel shims – a very time-onsuming job that brought criticism for the mount of attention it needed to keep the andling in trim. The final models used a much ore sensible screw adjustment that requires the se of a small tool in the kit. It takes barely half n hour to set it up to taste, balancing vibrations om the transmission against handling quality.

The primary chain is adjusted automatically istead of moving the gearbox to tension the nain, and the rear wheel really is quickly etachable.

Overall fuel consumption averaged 36 mpg, ut a tune-up and tappet adjustment (just like the ld days) before the MIRA test session improved nis to 42·5 mpg for the final tankful. Oil used nproved to 580 mpp at 1,800 miles from new.

In its Manx Norton-type finish of silver with ed and black lining, the Commando is as andsome as ever with plenty of polished alloy nd chrome.

It is sad that production of the Commando /as stopped so soon with such a loyal following f riders.

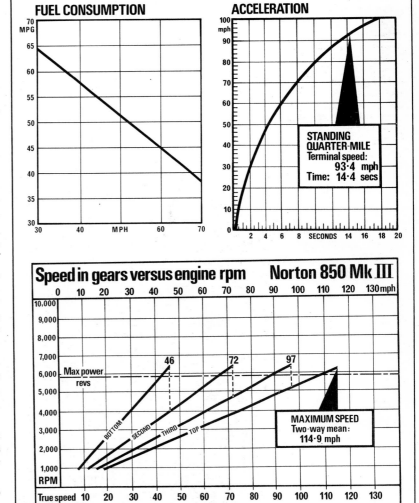

Suzuki GT750M

Suzuki, like Kawasaki, were slow to produce a large capacity roadster in answer to Honda's CB750 four. But when they did, early in 1972, it was a stunner. As expected of a factory with an already strong line of two-strokes and a reputation for thorough design and conservative styling, the Suzuki GT750 was an extension of the theme but with new twists that gave the bike a definite edge.

It was a three-cylinder machine, like the Kawasaki 750 that appeared the same year, but from there on the two machines diverged in completely opposite directions. Where the Kawasaki was a harsh, untamed and indecently fast, the Suzuki sniffed back with the grand touring image that its model number suggested. It was big, bulky, luxurious and gentlemanly; a mach-ine for quiet and unobtrusively fast travel.

It was also uniquely Suzuki. Today we acce that the big four Japanese manufacturers pr duce very similar machines in a variety of classe But in 1972 each factory was able to follow own style; Suzuki's was the development of th sophisticated two-stroke engine, and in th GT750 they took it to the limit.

With all three cylinders housed in a jacket, th GT750 engine was liquid cooled with a massi radiator spanning the front of the engine, th liquid being circulated by a mechanical pump the bottom of the broad crankcases. To make th engine narrower, the porting was canted to o side, giving an asymmetric appearance to th three exhaust pipes.

To give the engine and cycle parts a sli

Below: the Suzuki GT750M was much faster than the earlier water-cooled threes but still needed respect on twisty roads
Far right: the GT750A had slightly restyled tank graphics

istline, the gearbox was narrowed by taking e drive from the built-up crankshaft by gears the inner side of the right-hand side cylinder. brication was Suzuki's patented system with a arbox-driven pump supplying the cylinder lls and main bearings with oil from a tank der the seat. To allow for variations in load, e oil input was varied according to the throttle ening, a cable from the twistgrip altering the row of the pump.

For the ruggedness of its engineering, the big zuki was modestly tuned. Three 32-mm choke rburettors fed the simple porting and on a rected compression ratio of 6·7 to 1 the 738 cc gine developed a claimed 67 bhp at 6,500 rpm. w accurate that figure was is neither here nor ere, for the great virtue of the GT750 was its xibility. With a muted drone from the four haust pipes (the middle cylinder fed a bifur- ted pair of silencers underneath the two outer pes), the big Suzy would pull like a train from w revs and this made the five-speed gearbox ther superfluous. But it was all in character. e suspension was soft and mushy and the nited ground clearance afforded by the bulky haust system further discouraged spirited rnering.

It was slow too, an aspect of the bike that was stand out for some time despite the successful cing efforts of the factory using tuned versions the engine developing over 100 bhp and pable of over 170 mph.

In a period when most seven fifties were pable of reaching nearly 120 mph, the GT750 s unable to top 110 mph and its weight (nearly 0 lb) prevented startling acceleration. Neither s its fuel consumption impressive.

Run the bike at anything like its maximum uising speed of 90 mph, which it would be able do smoothly and reliably for as long as the ler could manage the rather ungainly riding sition, and the three big 32-mm choke Mikuni rburettors would guzzle fuel at an alarming te; 25 mpg would not be unusual and this awback was only partially overcome by the e of the fuel tank. In these days when disc akes are becoming increasingly criticised for eir poor wet performance, the stopping equip- ent on the early GT750s would please many a ng-distance tourer; a double-leading shoe, uble-sided drum unit no less! But it failed to eet the promise of its appearance and repeated ops from speed would provoke fade easily.

Apart from boosting the braking power with a ir of massive discs on the front wheel (albeit th a disclaimer stuck to the front fork warning the delay in their wet weather potency), Suzuki peared rather happy for the GT750 to retain podgy character for three years.

With the introduction of the GT750M in 1975 at all changed. Suddenly here was a Suzuki at could take on the best superbikes and come t on top. Compared to the old model it looked isp, lean and hungry, although it was still a rmidable machine for fast riding. Porting anges, which were the most significant modifi-

cations to the bike, boosted the power to 70 bhp at 6,500 rpm. Gone was the electric fan behind the radiator (meant for tropical climates only) and the exhaust system was cleaned up and more tidily tucked into the running gear. Three massive 40-mm choke constant-velocity carbur- ettors with a single control cable allowed deeper breathing for the chunky motor.

The alterations had had the desired effect, transforming the podgy tourer into a drag strip flyer. In its new guise, the GT750 wound up to 120 mph mean top speed on test and sprinted through the standing quarter-mile in 13·5 sec, terminating at 100 mph.

This increase in performance was achieved with little sacrifice of the bike's high-speed touring character. The GT750 is as tireless, smooth and comfortable as ever. Better still, the fuel con- sumption was improved. Although one of the better two-strokes in this respect, and even though most of the test mileage was clocked on motorways, overall consumption during our test was 37·7 mpg, while the lowest figure recorded – during the flat out MIRA test session – was a remarkable 33·3 mpg. And all on low-grade fuel too.

But while the engine has been improved with lengthened port timing, bigger constant-velocity Mikuni carburettors, higher compression ratio and the overall gearing raised, the chassis has remained little changed. The handling has not kept pace with the increased performance; this is not too great a problem as the cornering clearance, although vastly improved since the earlier models, still puts the dampers on any

spirited riding. The GT750 now has an identity crisis too. The bike still looks a podgy tourer with its massive silencers, four in all, and this could have discouraged potential customers although the bike represented the best value for money in the 750 cc class, considering its all-round performance.

It could also put them off experiencing one of the more thrilling seven fifties. Blip the light-weight throttle and the crank spins instantaneously in response. The flywheels are so light and the engine so free moving that it sounds and feels more like a small two-stroke twin.

Specification

Engine: 738 cc (70 × 64 mm) water-cooled, two-stroke, in-line three. Linered light-alloy cylinder block and head. Four ball main bearings; needle-roller big ends. Lubrication by throttle-controlled pump to main bearings and cylinder bores. Compression ratio, 6·9 to 1 (from exhaust port closure). Three 40 mm Mikuni CV carburettors with lever-operated cold-start jets; paper element air filter. Claimed maximum power 70 bhp at 6,500 rpm.

Transmission: Primary helical gears. Wet, multiplate clutch and five-speed gearbox. Overall ratios: 12·8, 7·81, 6·13, 5·06 and 4·33 to 1. Final chain, 0·625 × 0·375 in. Mph at 1,000 rpm in top gear, 17.

Electrical Equipment: Coil ignition. 12-volt, 14-amp-hour battery and 280-watt excited field alternator and voltage regulator. 6·5-in headlamp with 50/40-watt main bulb. Starter motor; direction indicators; headlamp flasher; gear position indicator.

Brakes: Hydraulically-operated twin 11·75 in diameter front discs; 7·5 in drum rear.

Tires: Avon Roadrunner, 4·10 × 19 in front, 4·10 × 18 in rear.

Suspension: Telescopic front fork. Pivoted rear fork with three-position spring preload adjustment.

Frame: Welded duplex tube with pressed plate gusseting.

Dimensions: Wheelbase, 58·75 in; seat height, 31 in; ground clearance, 6 in; all unladen.

Weight: Approximately 550 lb.

Fuel Capacity: 4·5 gals including reserve.

Oil Tank Capacity: 3·8 pts.

Manufacturer: Suzuki Motor Co., 300 Takatsuka, Hamamatsu, Japan.

Performance

Maximum Speeds (Mean): 119·8 mph; 110·2 mph with rider seated normally.

Best One-way Speed: 120·4 mph – dry track, hot with slight cross wind.

Braking Distance – from 30 mph: 30 ft 6 in.

Fuel Consumption: 37·7 mpg.

Oil Consumption: 290 mpp overall.

Minimum Non-snatch Speed: 14 mph in top gear.

Speedo Accuracy:

Indicated mph	20	30	40	50	60	70	80	90	100
Actual mph	19	28·6	37·6	46·5	55·6	64·7	74·4	84	93·8

With the new porting the power characteristics have been completely transformed. What was formerly a tourquey engine is now a revver. Little power is developed below 4,000 rpm, although it will pull usefully for town work. Opening the throttles produces little more than a moan from the air filter, but as the revs build up and reach 4,000 rpm the bike shoots forward and the engine whirrs like a turbine as the maximum power revs at 6,500 rpm are reached.

With such a reduction in flexibility you might expect the touring ability of the Suzuki to be hampered. But the gearbox ratios – apart from the large gap from bottom to second where the revs drop from 7,000 to 4,200 – are adequately close when the gear pedal is used vigorously.

The high-speed cruising character of the GT750, one of its great strengths, has also not been lost in the change. Just attain the speed you want – anything up to 100 mph – and the big

Suzy will hold it for you as long as you war
Even at high speeds the 750 has a range of 1
miles before reserve, and more with the bigg
tank of the later GT750A. And at these sort
speeds there is plenty in hand. Just a shade off t
stop is needed to maintain 70 mph and at 5,00
rpm (90 mph) in top tweaking the grip produce
healthy kick for overtaking.

Except for a pronounced chain noise at spee
engine noise levels are remarkably low too, b
engine vibration intrudes into the picture abo
70 mph sufficiently to buzz the footrests and se
the rider's feet to sleep. This is in spite of t
three-cylinder engine, which by nature produc
a side to side rocking vibration, being mounted
rubber bushes. In general use this vibration go
unnoticed apart from around the marked reso
ance period at 7,000 rpm, when the shaking
clearly visible.

Starting and idling belie the Suzuki's hi
power capabilities. Without a sound it respon
instantly to the starter button and relaxes into
reliable, if slightly irregular sounding tickov
(difficult to persuade down to 1,000 rpm witho
putting up with the occasional stalling).

The clutch is as smooth and light as ever b
the gearbox has the same annoying Suzu
characteristics. Bottom gear was rarely engag
noiselessly, particularly if the rear chain need
adjustment, and selection of the lower rati
nearly always felt clonky. Otherwise the gearbo
which has had the top two ratios closed up
that there is now only a 1,200 rpm drop betwee
the two, felt perfectly crisp. Particularly usef
for telling a rider he has reached top gear is t
digital gear indicator in the instrument conso
As each ratio is selected then the relative numb
is shown. If this not necessarily a must for
modern bike it does indicate the level to whi
Suzuki has refined its instrumentation.

Both the 160 mph speedo and rev counter a
lit at night by a cosy green glow; between the
are the warning lights and water temperatu
gauge, which never wavered over 'cool'.

Controls have never been bettered on
Suzuki. As for the overall comfort of the bike, t
hand controls have been refined to the poi
where they are no longer noticed. What is need
is there, instantly, but I would prefer contr
levers that were thicker, particularly for t
brake lever as this requires heavy pressu
although it was good to see the rubber cover ov
the cable end.

In spite of the very wide engine (28 in) t
riding comfort is good. The seat is long and wi
and the flat handlebar gives the rider a go
stance at high speed while remaining relaxed
low speed.

The suspension could be improved howeve
While the front fork has a pleasantly soft b
slightly underdamped action, the rear suspensi
units transmitted too much of the small ro
ripples and were overdamped. The effect w
very annoying over badly surfaced roads
practically everything was transmitted to t
rider while the bigger bumps only were absorbe

...en Roadrunner tires were fitted front and ...r instead of the standard Bridgestones. If ...ything, they improved the steering at low ...eds due to the large rolling diameter of the ...e increasing the self-centring action. The ...ering lightens as you lean the bike over and ...ove onto the more curved section of the tread ...the side walls, a characteristic which was un-...rving at first. In addition, the whole machine ...els less than stable at anything over 90 mph. ...There is also a ground clearance problem. The ...encers have been lifted up but the wide main ...d prop stands still crunch down at only ...oderate lean angles.

In contrast the braking is superb. The twin ...wer at the expense of heavy lever action . . . in ...e dry. What happens in the wet at slow speeds ...unknown as it never rained during the test, but ...zuki are obviously aware of some short-...mings and they say so by warning owners with ...sticker on the front fork leg. It is just as well ...ere is a decent drum rear brake.

...Lighting, which does not include a pilot bulb ...the headlamp, is ample for the legal limit. ...The tools are sufficient for the tasks most ...ners will use them for, the only attention our ...st bike needing being to lift the seat and refill ...e oil tank, the lubricant for which was used at ...0 miles to the pint, giving a range of over 1,000 ...iles, and one adjustment of the rear chain in the ...me period.

...The GT750, which was dropped from the ...zuki range at the end of 1977, was a healthy ...ternative to the faster four-stroke GS750 four, ...en if dated in its handling and comfort. Had it ...ot been for exhaust emission control laws it ...ight still be with us.

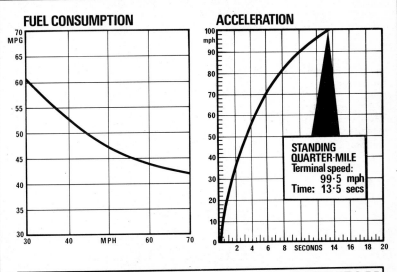

FUEL CONSUMPTION

ACCELERATION

STANDING QUARTER-MILE
Terminal speed: 99·5 mph
Time: 13·5 secs

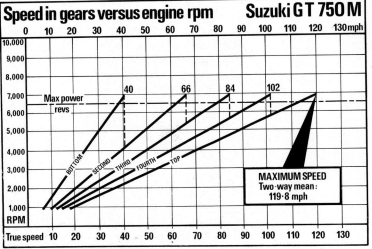

Speed in gears versus engine rpm   **Suzuki GT 750 M**

Max power revs

40   66   84   102

BOTTOM   SECOND   THIRD   FOURTH   TOP

MAXIMUM SPEED
Two-way mean: 119·8 mph

Suzuki
RE5

With the generally overwhelming success of the Japanese motor cycle industry it is all too easy to forget the disasters. For there were the lemons, and along with Yamaha's ill-fated and unreliable TX750 ohc twin, Suzuki's foray into the rotary-engine field with the RE5 was the most disastrous of the lot.

We write of the RE5 in the past tense because after its introduction in late 1974, production lasted only two years and with slight simplifications in the specification faultered toward its demise in mid-summer 1977.

By all the criteria, the RE5 was a superbi[ke] despite all its faults. It was big, smooth and if n[ot] actually capable of blinding acceleration throu[gh] the quarter mile, offered the rider a flexi[ble] engine and short-burst super-smooth high spe[ed] cruising.

The main reasons for its failure were fund[a]mental as well as obvious. Outlandish it certai[n] was, too outlandish in appearance and sou[nd]. But basically it could not deliver the goods. [Its] performance profile almost mirrored the chea[p] GT550 two-stroke three while offering noth[ing] more in excitement and image.

Four years of development went into Japa[n's] first entry into the rotary-bike arena a[nd] Suzuki's first attack into the ultra-luxury bi[ke] field. Millions of miles in conditions that vari[ed] from arctic to desert were covered during t[he] factory road testing period.

Suzuki obviously had considerable confide[nce] in it, for they invested millions in the program[me] along with a new factory specially built for t[he] sole purpose of rotary production.

Anything but a remarkable machine fr[om] such massive investment would have come as [a] surprise, and the RE5 was certainly that. [A] combination of Italian and Japanese styling s[et] off the massive alloy rotary engine-transmissi[on] unit that was tightly packed into the frame.

In typical Japanese fashion, Suzuki built in[to] the RE5 every conceivable design feature [to] remove any possibility of criticism. Unfortu[n]ately, it resulted in an extremely heavy machi[ne]. Fully tanked up, it weighed a fantastic 560 [lb]. Even with just over one gallon of fuel it tipp[ed] the scales at more than the previously heavie[st] Jap machine, the Kawasaki 900 four. This [is] certainly remarkable when you remember t[he] claims made for the Wankel engine during [its] infancy, of its relative compactness for a giv[en] capacity, light weight and smoothness.

There is no doubt about the rotary's virtu[es] and of the Suzuki RE5 engine, particularly. As [a] motor cycle power unit, it was the silkie[st] mechanically quietest and one of the mo[st] flexible yet seen.

More in line with contemporary Wanke[l]

…vered cars, the RE5 had a water-cooled casing …the motor and a cooling radiator very similar …he Suzuki GT750 two-stroke three. This also …orporated an electric fan, a feature dropped …the later model.

…he rotor itself was cooled by the rotor shaft …ricant supplied by an Eaton-type pump from …sump under the engine unit, coolant circul-…ng to an additional radiator beneath the water …iator.

…he rotor tips were lubricated, two-stroke …hion, by a throttle-controlled pump supplied …m a tank under the seat. Both lubricating …tems used the same oil but were entirely …arate from each other.

…ransmission was by a duplex chain to a …ltiple plate clutch and the GT750 gearbox.

…or a motor cycle powered by a unit supposed …be less complicated and more compact than …uivalent multi-cylinder engines, the RE5 was …ghteningly complex. The carburettor, for …mple, had two pairs of push-pull cables plus a …le for the oil pump. The whole carburettor …embly required exceptionally careful setting …for the best results.

…Where the RE5 was best, it was head-and-…oulders above the competition. It could cruise, …ooth as glass and silent as a whisper, at speeds …und 100 mph.

…or a seasoned motor cyclist this can be a …lly strange experience. Like the Norton-…umph rotary prototype, the Suzuki added a …w dimension to autobahn travel and the …uctions the smoothness can make to rider …igue over long periods are much more than …e would expect.

…Suzuki have always been aware of the need for …er comfort, as has been ably demonstrated by …their smaller machines, and they went even …ther with the RE5. Even though it is a massive …chine overall, the seat was low and slim and …st people had no problems in putting both feet …t on the ground when stationary. Flattish …ndlebars and nicely placed footpegs, mounted …t aft of the seat nose, completed the picture. …n contrast, you need to be a champion weight …er to pull the bike up on to its main stand, so …orly arranged is the foot lever on the stand.

…Although top end performance was less than …nning, since Suzuki's 750 three can easily …tpace the RE5 over the quarter-mile, the …tary impressed mainly for its stump-pulling …wer at low revs and wide range of flexibility. …Throttle response was startling at the maxi-…um torque revs of 3,500 rpm and twisting the …p really stretched a rider's arms before he …lised that the bike was whistling toward the …l line at 7,000 rpm.

…Such a wide range of engine torque made the …ful top gear range very broad and had it not …en for the high tickover speed of 1,500 rpm, it …ght have been even better. The pulling ability …the RE5 was so hard that it could comfortably …e a 1-in-3 test hill at 1,500 rpm in bottom gear …d pull away at little more than this.

…This, more than anything, accentuated the unusual exhaust note emitted by the RE5. At speed, the massive silencers with the 'Ram Air' cooling injectors at the front ends damped out the sharp exhaust notes into a hollow hum that hardly turned an ear. Below 4,000 rpm, used quite often, the notes from the single rotor sounded more like a cross between a Norton ES2 single and a Villiers two-stroke. And the 'pokity-pokity' racket was particularly resonant when one was pulled up beside cars at traffic lights.

One regrettable feature of the complex carbur-ettor set-up meant that the model we tested was slightly below par – not enough to affect the maximum performance, but sufficient to spoil the light-throttle response of the two carburettor chokes, one of 18-mm and the other of 32-mm, the smaller of which have small ports with later timing ports for better filling at low revs.

Up to about 40 per cent of twistgrip move-ment, the smaller choke opens with no effect on the larger at all and response is quite sluggish. From there, the main choke takes over and the engine becomes much more lively. The vacuum-operated constant-velocity 32-mm choke could be beaten by a slick wrist and the engine would cough. Such a lag was also apparent in the vacuum sensing of the over-run ignition that fires the plug at half speed to prevent rough running on closed throttle.

Far left: *the Suzuki Rotary RE5A was sold in limited numbers with many components similar to the two-stroke GT750 three. In its original form* (below) *it had futuristic styling*

Until the ignition cut in a fraction of a second after shutting the throttle, quite considerable engine braking effect showed, sometimes with a discernible squeal from the rear tyre in low gears.

But then there came a deathly silence when the engine ran on without any braking effect at all, a characteristic that needed getting used to.

For all its refinement, the Suzuki demonstrated appalling fuel consumption figures.

Specification

Engine: Single-rotor, transversely-mounted, Wankel type; water-cooled casing and oil-cooled rotor; 497 cc chamber volume. Rotorshaft lubricated by Eaton-type pump; sump capacity, 4·5 pts. Rotor tips lubricated by throttle-controlled pump; tank capacity, 3·6 pts. Compression ratio, 9·4 to 1. Mikuni HHD carburettor with 18 mm primary and 32 mm secondary ports; lever-operated choke; oil-soaked polyurethane air filter. Claimed maximum power, 62 bhp at 6,500 rpm.

Transmission: Primary drive by 0·375 in pitch double-row chain with automatic tensioner. Wet, multiplate clutch and five-speed gearbox. Overall ratios: 14·44, 8·81, 6·91, 5·71 and 4·68 to 1. Final drive by 0·75 × 0·375-in type 630 chain with throttle-controlled pump lubrication. Mph at 1,000 rpm in top gear, 16·7.

Electrical Equipment: Capacitor-discharge assisted coil ignition. 12-volt, 24-amp-hour battery and 280-watt alternator. 7-in diameter headlamp with 50/40-watt main bulb. Direction indicators; starter motor; headlamp flasher; coolant temperature gauge.

Brakes: Hydraulically-operated 11·75-in diameter double-disc front; 7-in SLS drum rear.

Tires: Inoue Grand High Speed, 3·25 × 19-in ribbed front, 4·00 × 18-in patterned rear; light-alloy rims.

Suspension: Telescopic front fork with two-way damping. Pivoted rear fork with five-position spring preload adjustment.

Frame: Duplex loop cradle.

Dimensions: Wheelbase, 59 in; seat height, 32 in; ground clearance, 7·5 in; overall length, 81 in; turning circle, 17 ft; all unladen.

Weight: 560 lb with one gallon of fuel.

Fuel Capacity: 4·3 gals including reserve.

Manufacturer: Suzuki Motor Company, 300 Takatsuka, Hamamatsu.

Performance

Maximum Speed (Mean): 110 mph.
Best One-way Speed: 116 mph – damp track, strong three-quarter tail wind.
Braking Distance: Not taken due to damp track.
Fuel Consumption: 33·3 mpg overall.
Minimum Non-snatch Speed: 25 mph in top gear.
Speedo Accuracy:

Indicated mph	20	30	40	50	60	70	80	90	100
Actual mph	18	27	37	48	59	69	79	89	99

Overall, but including a large proportion motorway running, the RE5 recorded 25 m and even with careful throttle use it showed 33·3 mpg.

That sort of figure might have been accepta to a rich buyer but for the fact that capacity of RE5 tank was only 4·2 gallons. As a long dista tourer, the RE5 was sorely handicapped wit range of less than 110 miles. Moreover, capacity before the reserve tap was needed only 3 gallons and we rarely went 90 m before opening up again. This was necess because the low fuel warning lamp came on wh on reserve.

As well as refuelling, the bike needed filling with oil in the two locations, the sump using at 333 mpp, and the tank at 440 mpp.

The transmission was not quite up to the sa impressive standard as the engine. The gearb and clutch were typically Suzuki, being nigh perfect for lightness of action except for clonkiness in the action in the lower gears.

But Suzuki opted for the same heavy ¾-in pi chain as used on the Kawasaki 900. The m trouble was in the need to use a 14-tooth eng sprocket and this led to annoying vibrations the 4,000 to 4,500 rpm range.

On smooth dry roads the RE5 steered as v as any machine out of Japan. Slow turns in s streets and feet-up coasts to a stop can be jus well accomplished as high-speed bend swingi But the bike never gave the same degree confidence in its handling qualities as equival machines and this must to some extent be blam on its excessive weight and top heaviness.

The suspension had a short movement a gave a well-cushioned ride while at the same ti transmitting small ripples, rather like an ea Honda 750. But although well damped, the r spring units found trouble in controlling comparatively light rear end on bumpy corne

The main criticism was of the weight dis bution. Not only was the RE5 a heavy mach but the centre of gravity was high as well, and t was obvious to anyone who tried to manhan the bike.

For no apparent reason, apart perhaps fr cosmetics, the engine was placed very high up the frame, and this coupled with a high a heavy cooling system provided plenty of t hamper to limit spirited riding. It also ma riding in the wet a nightmare as the tyres w only average on wet surfaces.

Wet weather also took the bite out of the fr double disc brake – a characteristic whi should have been sorted out by a company w Suzuki's resources.

For all Suzuki's efforts in producing sophist ated and reliable electrical systems, the he light was poor too. There was plenty of pow from the plastic casing mounted unit but, like the smaller models, the dip beam dazzled t much due to the lack of adequate cut-off.

The instrumentation and detail work w fantastic. The cylindrical casing housing the l mph speedo and 9,000 rpm rev counter had

Far left: *the RE5's
instrument console had a
flip-up lid released when
the ignition was switched
on. In addition to the
coolant temperature
gauge and digital gear
indicator there was a
row of warning lamps
for fuel level, oil level,
neutral and main beam,
which could be checked
before firing up*
Left: *the unorthodox
engine with its dual
choke carburettor
forward of the rotor
casing*

ansparent green cover released when the
nition key next to it was switched on the
eckout position. When this was used, the
rcuits operating the various warning lamps
ere checked. The low fuel lamp, the low oil and
l pressure all came on alongside the turn-signal
peater, main beam and neutral bulbs.

Between the instruments are the gear-position
dicator and the coolant temperature gauge,
hich only went above the mid position when
nning at speed in dense motorway traffic.

Starting was absolutely simple. There was no
essing with the vacuum-operated fuel tap, the
nition switch was turned to the main position,
e choke lever on the carburettor pressed down
t is overridden at operating temperature) and a
ab on the starter button did the trick.

The basic styling was very pleasing but spoiled
y the unnecessary harping on the rotary idea
ith round casings for the rear lamp, instruments
d the side covers. But the detail work was
od, and typified by the extensive use of cap
rews, and neat light-alloy wheel rims.

As a serious motorcycle it is difficult to
nagine where the Suzuki RE5 fitted into the
cture. It was too heavy and not powerful
ough to be a sports machine, yet at the same
me its long distance touring potential was
arred by the heavy fuel consumption and
mited range. It was no doubt aimed at the
merican long distance tourer who would find
e utter smoothness and comfort a boon, if he
d not mind stopping for fuel every 100 miles.

Looked at in cold hard terms, the RE5 offered
ttle more than the GT550 Suzuki three at the
xpense of greater weight and fuel consumption,
where was the progress in that?

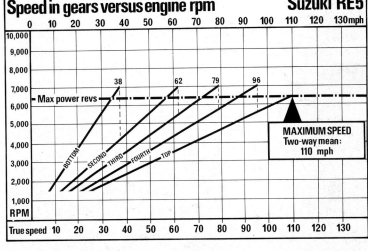

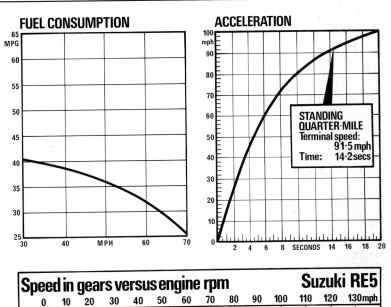

Suzuki GS750

With tough emmision controls in America pushing out Suzuki's top of the range water-cooled three-cylinder two-stroke GT750 at the end of 1977, the factory was bound to pull something exceptional out of the bag when they introduced their first large four-stroke machine. And when the four-cylinder GS750 appeared at the end of 1976, it proved to be not only the fastest seven-fifty on the market but the most compact and best mannered big bike to appear from Japan to that date. Most heavyweights are hard to handle when stationary and the Suzuki GS750 is no exception, but the factory engineers were bright enough to realise that what was needed in the 750 cc class was a machine with superior roadholding and manageability as w[ell] as more power.

What they came up with was a large mot[or]cycle (60-in wheelbase) with uncanny stabili[ty] for a Japanese bike at speed and with a remar[k]ably low all-up weight of 510 lb when most 750[cc] machines weighed around 540 lb. They mi[ni]mised the effects of bulk by clever frame desig[n] that allowed a low seat height. The high pow[er] output of the engine developed a claimed 68 b[hp] at 8,500 rpm.

By the standards of the day – Honda lat[er] replied with their equally fast CB750F2 – the t[op] speed of the GS750 was a revelation. Clocked a[t] a mean two-way top speed of 124·3 mph it w[as]

e fastest 750 cc machine ever tested by *Motor cle*.

Acceleration was no less stunning. Despite a or rear tire that limited traction in full-ooded drag style starts, the Suzuki catapulted 60 mph from rest in under 4 sec – and can top 0 mph in under 13 sec.

For such performance the low overall fuel nsumption is impressive too. Average for the st was just under 42 mpg while the bike was able return 39·1 mpg when cruising at 70 mph on otorways.

Yet mechanically, the Suzuki is very con-ntional by contemporary standards. The four-linder 748 cc short stroke (65 by 56·4 mm) has ouble-overhead camshafts with chain drive and built-up all-roller bearing crankshaft and gear imary drive that is a virtual copy of the awasaki 900 four, right down to valve sizes and e way inverted bucket followers with adjusting ims transmit camshaft thrust to the valves.

The frame is a well-braced duplex tube cradle ad there is nothing radical or different about the spension. Even the brakes follow fashion with stainless-steel disc front and rear. But Suzuki ave scored with the GS750 by absorbing every ate-of-the-art idea on handling and rider omfort into the context of the classic Japanese ulti. This shows immediately you slide into the at. The machine is very low (31½ in unladen) d just as important, the seat is slim, along with e side panels, and is padded enough to prevent knifing through you on long rides. Above all, e GS750 has a moulded-to-you feel that gives e rider confidence in the machine as soon as he under way. And he will need it, for the Suzuki ill out-accelerate just about anything on the ad up to the legal limit.

Yet at low speeds, trundling around town, the ay the bike can be weaved through the traffic elies none of the screaming performance and ce-bred roadholding that befits a machine arely a few steps removed from Suzuki's world hampionship winning RG500 two-stroke road acer.

The steering and balance are as carefree as the ontrols are smooth and light, and the machine els no heavier than the smaller Suzuki GT380 wo-stroke. It makes the GS750 a joy to de – unlike many Japanese heavyweights.

That is nothing compared to the thrill of ranking the big Suzy through fast bends. You el as if you are piloting a responsive fighter ircraft. Squirt it, and the Suzy goes like a jet. im it and you have suddenly got an accurate issile in your hands.

The Suzuki engineers have tuned the steering o finely that it becomes taut at speed yet retains useful amount of neutrality for flicking through orners with a minimal amount of effort from the ider.

While the steering geometry is certainly spot n, the frame itself contributes no less to the verall picture. Although very similar to the Kawasaki duplex frame, the Suzuki version is berally gusseted around the steering head and

between the three top tubes for extra stiffness, while the swinging arm bearings are needle rollers to minimise wear and flexure.

It makes the Suzuki the scratcher's dream. The four exhaust pipes are routed into a single silencer on each side, and this offers cornering clearance which means that the Suzuki invites taste on normal roads.

Unfortunately the tires and the rear sus-pension are not up to the standard of the rest of the running gear. The stock-issue Bridgestones are possibly long-lasting, but are the first to signal warnings on smooth surfaces, while the 120 lb/in rear springs are too hard for the dampers and start to bounce the rear end around on ripply tarmac. This is enough to provoke a slight side-to-side steering head motion above 90 mph.

The ride comfort suffers too, for even on apparently smooth roads the Suzuki bounces along perceptibly at the rear. Yet by comparison the front fork is superb. The soft 26/43 lb/in dual rate springs are just right and the fork gives a beautifully smooth ride; although the damping is apparently light, it works well in practice.

For long distance cruising the flat handlebar offers a neat riding posture that balances the wind pressure up to 80 mph. It would be even better with slightly more sweep on the handlebar and the footrests an inch or two further back.

Unless ridden hard with the engine revving to its 10,000 rpm limit, the Suzuki is commendably smooth too. Throughout the range, the engine

emits a high-frequency buzz which is at its worst when the motor is taken over 6,000.

It is much more comfortable than the two-stroke 750 cc Suzuki three and the other big four-stroke fours, although not quite up to the standard of a BMW or the Yamaha 750 cc three, except at 5,000 in top (around 70 mph) when it is mirror smooth.

Since the Suzuki's mirrors are rubber mounted they are never affected by vibration.

Average consumption was 38·9 mpg on the cheapest fuel with almost 45·8 mpg when ridden carefully, or a worst figure of 27·5 mpg at the test track.

Mechanical noise is low and flexibility superb. At 30 mph in top it just hums along wi no more than a slight hiss from the valve gea but wind back the twistgrip and the bike will ki you straight up to a genuine 108 mph (115 m indicated) without a single gearchange with t rider sitting bolt upright. With the rider flat the tank, there is much more. Geared perfec on its 5·6 to 1 top ratio the GS750 revved in top 9,200 rpm, 300 rpm below the red line, for a tw way mean top speed of 124·3 mph.

Snap throttle is good provided there are mo than 3,000 rpm on the tacho, below which t engine is perfectly tractable but unresponsive full bore treatment.

The stunning road performance owes as mu to the engine power as to the optium geari used. The five-speed gearbox is as expected fro Suzuki, slick, positive and noiseless, unless yo try to perform quick changes at low engine rev when it becomes a mite clunky. Overall gearing comparatively low, and the buzzy feel of th engine often provoked the rider to feel f another gear ratio after top. The gear indicator the instrument panel for once proved useful this case. But the low gearing enhances th flexibility. In bottom gear, at 15·1 to 1 ratio, th bike will trickle along at little more than a casu walking pace, yet it tops out at 48 mph. T ratios are properly spaced, keeping the engi above peak torque revs (7,000 rpm) rig through the range when revved to 9,500 rpm. B in everyday use the most useful gear is thi which can leap the bike from 40 mph to 70 mp for instant overtaking.

The effect showed best at the test strip. Despi the lack of traction from the Bridgestone re tire, the Suzuki realed off a series of quarte miles at 13·2 sec with a terminal speed of 103 mph.

Yet it came back with barely a ruffled feathe The clutch is light and smooth yet bites without trace of slip, the exhaust pipes were as tarnis free as if they had just come off the spares shel and there was no trace of oil anywhere.

Braking during the tests at MIRA showed th Suzuki's 11¾-in discs to be very potent and fad free from 30 mph in the dry with a stoppin distance of under 26 ft. But in normal use the

Specification

Engine: 749 cc (65 × 56·4 mm) double-overhead camshaft, in-line, transverse four. Light-alloy cylinder head and block; cast-iron liners. Three roller and one ball main bearings; needle-roller big ends. Wet sump lubrication; trochoid pump. Compression ratio, 8·7 to 1. Four 26-mm choke Mikuni carburettors with lever-operated cold-start jets; oil-soaked foam air filter. Maximum claimed power, 68 bhp at 8,500 rpm. Maximum torque, 44 lb-ft at 7,000 rpm.

Transmission: Spur primary gears (ratio, 99/46). Wet, multiplate clutch and five-speed gearbox. Overall ratios: 15·1, 10·5, 8·12, 6·62 and 5·65 to 1. Final drive by 0·75 × 0·5-in roller chain (ratio 41/15). Mph at 1,000 rpm in top gear, 13·5.

Electrical Equipment: Twin coil ignition. 12-volt, 14-amp-hour battery and three-phase alternator with zener-diode voltage control. 7-in diameter headlamp with 50/40 watt main bulb. One fuse. Starter motor; direction indicators; gear position indicator.

Brakes: Hydraulically-operated 11·75-in diameter stainless-steel disc front and rear; single-piston caliper front, double rear.

Tires: Bridgestone, 3·25H19 ribbed 21 F2 front, 4·00H18 patterned 21 R2 rear.

Suspension: Telescopic front fork; 6·3 in travel. Pivoted rear fork; spring damper units with 3·3 in travel, and five-position preload adjustment.

Frame: Welded duplex tube cradle.

Dimensions: Wheelbase, 59 in; seat height, 31·5 in; ground clearance, 7 in; handlebar width, 29 in; castor angle, 63°; trail, 4·2 in; turning circle, 15 ft 10 in; all unladen.

Weight: 510 lb including one gallon of fuel.

Fuel Capacity: 4·8 gals including 4·8 pts reserve.

Sump Oil Capacity: 7·8 pts.

Manufacturer: Suzuki Motor Co. Ltd., 300 Takatsuka, Hamamatsu.

Performance

Maximum Speeds (Mean): 124·3 mph; 108·4 with normally-seated rider in two-piece over-suit.

Best One-way Speed: 125·3 mph — dry track, no wind.

Braking Distance — from 30 mph: 25 ft 6 in on dry tarmac.

Fuel Consumption: 38·9 mpg.

Oil Consumption: 500 mpp.

Minimum Non-snatch Speed: 15 mph in top gear.

Speedo Accuracy:

Indicated mph	30	40	50	60	70	80	90
Actual mph	26·6	35·3	44·1	52·3	60·5	72·0	83·7

Like the Kawasaki Z1000, the Suzuki GS750 has double overhead cams and a roller and ball bearing crankshaft with gear drive to the clutch and five-speed gearbox. The 1,000 cc version recently introduced is no wider and in fact shorter and lighter than the seven fifty

ere generally poor. The rear disc was far too sensitive from higher speeds and tended to overheat causing hopping of the rear wheel. Both rakes exhibited lag when used in heavy rain, the usual fault of stainless-steel discs.

Instrumentation and lighting were only average on the GS750. Speedometer and rev counter re in a new-style package that cants each instrument towards the rider's view. Unusually, ey had red illumination which became distracting after a while. A higher standard of accuracy from the needles would have been preferable. The headlamp sends out a strong eam and the dip cut off is much better than uzukis in the past. The left switch console is wkward because the headlamp flasher button is ricky to find.

The electric starting is so reliable now that it eems hardly worth a mention. Neat, though, is ne easy control of warm up idling speed by the old start lever, particularly as the GS750 is a bit old blooded.

The tool kit is small but effective and all the outine servicing is simple to perform. The air lters are washable foam and a check on oil level an be made through the sight glass on the clutch over.

Like Kawasaki, Suzuki have made the best of ne chain final drive without enclosing it. Each nk of the massive ¾-in pitch chain is sealed with)-rings and its adjustment at roughly 600 mile intervals, even in wet weather, was the only ttention the bike needed.

In performance, handling and comfort, the uzuki is almost top of its class first time out. ttention to the brakes could well make it erfect.

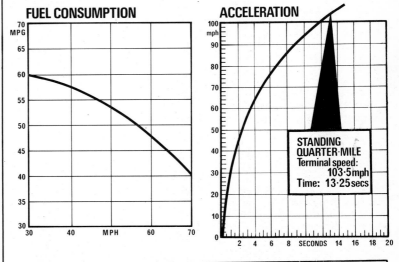

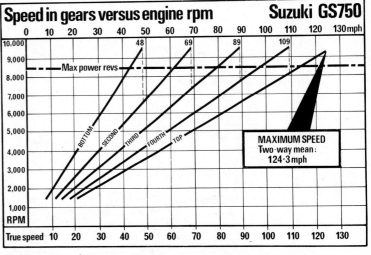

Triumph Trident T160

Few modern roadsters have a racing record as enviable as the Triumph Tridents and BSA Rocket Threes. American veteran Dick Mann used a BSA 750 cc three to win the Daytona 200 classic in 1970, John Cooper had some memorable wins at Mallory Park and Ontario, California, on a 750 cc Triumph and a production version took four wins on the trot in the Isle of Man Production TT.

However, it can be argued that the legend that these wins created lead to the downfall of the triples, for after development for racing by the fabled Doug Hele, the machines were very reliable, while the production versions were anything but that. It seemed that the factory were content to rest on their winner's laurels . . .

A result of the way it was derived from the 500 cc twin Triumph, the Trident was notoriously complex and costly to manufacture despite it only having pushrod valve operation. It was bugged by the old problems of oil leaks from the engine and front fork, even on the final T160.

This was the best triple made. It was fast, with a top speed of 120 to 125 mph and impeccable handling, while it boasted such up-to-da[te] features as electric starting, full instrumentatio[n] and a low and sleek profile.

It was undoubtedly one of the best lookin[g] Tridents made. In the classic Triumph mould [it] had a beautiful teardrop shape tank, swept bac[k] handlebars, a low seat and a pair of upswe[pt] silencers that set off the lines of the machi[ne] perfectly. Had it not been for the crippling cost [of] its manufacture and the unfortunate collapse [of] the Norton-Villiers-Triumph empire, the Tr[i]dents would still be rolling out of Small Heat[h.] As it is, manufacture stopped in late 1976.

The last Trident, the T160, boasted all th[e] features found on the earlier T150. The engi[ne] was a three-cylinder, set across the frame with th[e] two camshafts in the crankcases and pushrods t[o] the valves. A 120-degree spacing between th[e] crank throws gave the machine its distinctiv[e] exhaust note. Primary drive to the dry, sing[le] plate clutch was by a triplex chain. The gearbo[x] was the same five speed version found on the 65[0] and 750 twins. An electric starter drove th[e] engine through a ring gear on the clutch.

Major difference of the T160 was that the cylinders were canted forward in the interests of weight distribution, as on the BSA Rocket Three which went out of production in 1972.

The T160 was lower, sleeker and longer than the old T150 model and much more comfortable to ride. The changes to the bike started at the front forks which were lowered by using shorter springs. The mudguard had a plate mounting at the slider instead of the previous fragile tubular brackets.

The new instrument cluster with its warning lamps was bolted to the new top yoke.

The frame, derived from Les Williams' four-times Production TT-winner 'Slippery Sam' racer, was shallower overall but still allowed the engine to sit 1 in higher than before for better ground clearance and a lower seat height.

Specification

Engine: 740 cc (67 × 70 mm) overhead valve, transverse, in-line three. Light-alloy cylinder block and head. Four main bearings; two plain, one roller timing side, one ball drive side; plain big ends. Dry sump lubrication. Compression ratio, 9·5 to 1. Three 27-mm Amal carburettors with lever-operated air slides; paper-element air filter. Claimed maximum power, 58 bhp at 7,250 rpm.

Transmission: Duplex 0·437 in pitch primary chain with slipper tensioner. Dry single-plate clutch and five-speed gearbox. Overall ratios: 12·72, 9·04, 6·89, 5·85 and 4·92 to 1. Final drive by 0·625 × 0·375-in chain. Mph at 1,000 rpm, 15·5.

Electrical Equipment: Coil ignition with ballast resistor. 12-volt, 15-amp-hour battery and 120-watt alternator with zener-diode charge control. 7-in diameter headlamp with 45/40-watt main bulb. Starter motor, direction indicators.

Brakes: Hydraulically-operated 10-in diameter disc front and rear.

Tires: Dunlop TT100, 4·10 × 19-in front and rear.

Suspension: Telescopic front fork. Pivoted rear fork with three-position spring preload adjustment.

Frame: Duplex tube cradle with forged lugs.

Dimensions: Wheelbase, 59 in; seat height, 30·5 in; ground clearance, 6·5 in; overall length, 88 in; turning circle, 19 ft 6 in; all unladen.

Weight: 518 lb including one gallon of fuel.

Fuel Capacity: 5·75 gals.

Oil Tank Capacity: 7·2 pts.

Manufacturer: Norton Villiers Triumph Ltd, North Way, Walworth Industrial Estate, Andover, Hants.

Performance

Maximum Speeds (Mean): 119·5 mph; 100 mph with rider in two-piece outfit sitting normally.

Best One-way Speed: 124·8 mph – dry track, slight tail wind.

Braking Distance – from 30 mph: 27 ft 3 in.

Fuel Consumption: 31·3 gals overall.

Oil Consumption: 200 mpp.

Minimum Non-snatch Speed: 13 mph in top gear.

Speedo Accuracy:

Indicated mph	30	40	50	60	70	80	90	100
Actual mph	29·4	39·8	50·1	59·9	69·8	80·5	90·9	101

The rear fork lengthened by an inch, broug the wheelbase up to 59 in.

The Trident T160 really shows its mettle wh you stretch its legs on long, fast and bum bends. Despite rear spring rates that are on t soft side for good handling, the confidence a ease with which the T160 could be rushed alo without drama was marvellous.

Wet weather handling is even better. On t worst greasy roads the London suburbs cou offer, the Trident had fewer vices than most bik have in the dry. There is a natural stability to t machine that is almost uncanny.

The suspension and frame are not who perfect though. The rear fork has been weaken in its lengthening and this showed when it twist after hitting bumps with two-up. The front fo suffered hydraulic lock on sharp bumps a clonked loudly. There were also leaks from t slider seals, although this was to be corrected b better design.

Performance has changed little since t introduction of the original 1968 models. A though a three-into-two collector exhaust syste had been adopted to spread the mid-ran torque and cut noise levels, the three-cylind engine produces most of its torque in the top e of the rev range. It burbles along nicely a controllably at low revs but gives its best abo 4,500. It seemed to make hardly any differen whether you changed up at 7,000 or 8,0 rpm – the Trident surged along with just the same urgency.

Gearing is slightly lower than the original Tridents, but the latest model easily equalled the earlier ones on top-end speed. With a two-way mean of 119·5 mph and a best of almost 125 mph it makes the Trident one of the fastest machines in 1976.

In practice, however, the lack of low end torque did not reflect this potential. Sitting up in a two-piece outfit, the best the triple could achieve was a mean 100 mph in top gear. This was mainly because of the large gap between fourth and top was not matched to the power characteristics. With the gearbox a compromise derived from the twins it did not allow a fine adjustment of the gear ratios for optimum results. Nevertheless, the Trident is perfectly capable of sustaining an easy 90 mph two-up on the open road.

Engine vibration was not quite down to the levels of most four-cylinder machines, but at the same time was never worrying. There was a resonant patch around 4,500 rpm that is transmitted mainly through the footrests. Handlebars are rubber-mounted – the footrests should have been, too.

The gearchange is noiseless and slick, losing nothing in the change to the left side. Most changes on the move were clutchless but the dry clutch managed to lose its fine adjustment and slipped during the acceleration tests. Had the clutch been up to scratch, 0·2 seconds would have been cut from the quarter-mile time of 13·8 sec.

For general use the proportions of seat and handlebars are superb. With a height of only 30½ in the seat is low enough for all but the shortest to stand astride. It was long and well padded, too, with plenty of room for a passenger.

For fast riding however, the footrests are still too far forward, even though they have been moved back by 1 in on the left and 2 in on the right compared to the T150. The result is that, at any speed over 60 mph, too much weight is placed on the arms. The factory's answer is that they could not move the pegs back any farther because the kickstart lever is in the way.

The tank is a work of art. Beautifully styled, it holds over 5·5 gallons, useful as the Trident averaged a very poor 31·3 mpg in everyday use, giving a range of just over 170 miles. But when using premium fuel, some pinking was experienced at small throttle openings.

Oil consumption was similarly poor at 238 mpp, although much of this may have been due to the leaks from the primary chaincase and the rev-counter drive. The chaincase leak, from the clutch cable entry point, is caused by the drilling breaking into the inner casing. Owners can cure it by pressing a steel tube through into the clutch operating casing.

Starting from cold is reliable provided the rider floods each carburettor (the middle one by means of the lever, the others with the tickler buttons) and closes the air slides. Touching the button brings a resounding clunk as the staring

gear engages and the engines fires up.

The new thumb switches for the left hand are also a vast improvement on the old Lucas items but they suffered from internal corrosion of the contacts.

The Trident's braking is absolutely stunning. Once bedded in, both the front and rear Lockheed discs were capable of sensitive howling stops at the limit of the Dunlop TT100 tires' adhesion.

Hydraulics on the rear unit are much better than the Commando 850 Mark III, being tucked away behind the silencer mounts with the master cylinder filler under the seat.

Lighting, although only from a conventional 45/40-watt headlamp, is good enough for 60 mph riding at night. The dipped beam projected a strong fan-shaped beam with good cut-off.

Like all Triumphs, the Trident had a remarkably accurate speedo – within 1 mph correct up to 100 mph.

Typically British, the Trident demonstrates the skill of the development men to make the best of what is basically a crude modification of a smaller twin-cylinder machine. Had the management called for a design that started from scratch, Britain might have still had a strong industry.

A British classic, The Triumph Trident in its final T160 form was a thrilling machine to ride with fine handling and good top end power. Poor detail design spoilt it and industrial disasters killed it off

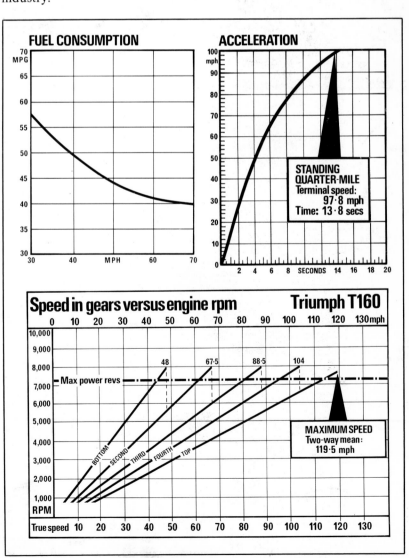

Triumph TR7RV Tiger 750

A lot of industrial history has been made since the then-new 744 cc Triumph Tiger was tested back in February of 1973. At that time it was being built at Meriden under the BSA-Triumph group banner: but that banner was already in tatters, and later in the year came the shotgun marriage with Norton Villiers.

Rightly or wrongly, the new management declared Meriden would be closed and sold, that Triumph twins were 'outdated' and would be dropped in favour of the more modern Nortons.

The outcome was the famous sit-in, and the ultimate formation of a workers' co-operative purchase and re-open the Meriden factory. T Bonneville 750 came back into production a now, Prince Charming has also kissed its sing carburettor cousin, the TR7RV Tiger 750.

Substantially (and understandably), the moc is as it was when put to sleep in 1973, with t only major changes a hydraulically-operated di brake instead of drum-type and, of course, t transfer of the gear pedal to the left side required by transatlantic regulations. There a too, later-pattern silencers, and a new a

ractive fuel-tank color scheme of deep bottle-
een and ivory.

Rather oddly, in the interim, the overall weight
checked on the MIRA weighbridge) appears
have crept up by around 30 lb, and not even
e makers can suggest a reason. Even so, at 448
the Tiger is still just about the lightest seven-
ty around, which is why it can give a very noble
count of itself, notwithstanding the fact that its
wer output of 49 bhp at 6,200 rpm is out-
nned by more exotic rivals.

It is unsophisticated – but relaxing with it. At
mph, the machine is merely ambling along, the
otor turning over lazily on little more than a
idgeon of throttle. This gait can be kept up for
ile after mile, hour after hour, with the
inimum of effort by rider or engine.

During the time the bike was in our hands, it
came in for a variety of uses, including motorway
dashes, a trip to the Victory Trial in mid-Wales, a
two-up tour, and general town and country
utility work. From all of this it emerged with a
38·3 mpg fuel consumption – rather disappoint-
ing, and some 10 mpg down on the correspond-
ing 1973 model.

No logical explanation could be found, but
possibly the pads of the disc brakes at front and
rear rub the surface lightly when in the 'off'
position and contribute to this increase in
consumption.

The use of front and rear disc brakes can be
regarded as an advance when applied to racing
bikes – but they seem hardly necessary on this
type of roadster, for they perform no better than

*Triumph fan Bob Currie,
Midland Editor of*
Motor Cycle, *takes the
Tiger 750 for a spin near
its home, the Meriden
factory near Nuneaton in
Warwickshire*

Following pages: *Sports
version of the TR7RV
Tiger 750 – the
Bonneville 750*

117

good twin-leading-shoe drum brakes. The TR7RV's stopping figure from 30 mph was a quite commendable 30 ft 4 in. However, the same model stopped in 30 ft when fitted with a rear drum brake.

On the road, a two-finger stroke of the lever was enough to cut the speed, and at the same time the disc gave a slightly more positive feel to the rear brake pedal. But it is all a matter of what one gets used to, and there will still be a strong body of unconvinced sceptics.

So how did the discs perform in rain? There

though, slick and positive.

One thing the Tiger can provide is a helping of power from way low down, and t shows up in the acceleration figures; around sec for a standing quarter-mile from a 'cooki seven-fifty cannot be bad!

For the standing quarter-mile, we gave it whole dragster treatment — lean-forward star smoky, snaking getaway. Wheelies, even. Ho ever, we were not impressed with the alm knobbly tread of the standard K70 rear tire a reckon we could have got better figures with

Specification

Engine: 744 cc (76 × 82 mm) overhead valve, parallel twin. Light-alloy cylinder head; cast-iron block. Roller drive-side, ball timing-side main bearings; plain big ends. Dry sump lubrication; piston pump. Compression ratio, 7·9 to 1. Amal 30-mm choke carburettor with lever-operated cold-start slide. Claimed maximum power, 46 bhp at 6,200 rpm. Maximum torque, 42 lb-ft at 5,300 rpm.
Transmission: Triplex 0·375-in pitch primary chain. Wet, multiplate clutch and five-speed gearbox. Overall ratios: 12·25, 8·63, 6·58, 5·59 and 4·7 to 1. Final drive by 0·625 × 0·375-in chain. Mph at 1,000 rpm in top gear, 16·1.
Electrical Equipment: Coil ignition. 12-volt, 10-amp-hour battery with charging by alternator, rectifier and zener diode. 7-in diameter headlamp with 45/40-watt main bulb.
Brakes: Hydraulically-operated 10-in diameter disc front and rear.
Tires: Dunlop Gold Seal K70, 3·25 × 19-in front, 4·00 × 18-in rear.
Suspension: Telescopic front fork. Pivoted rear fork with three-position spring preload adjustment and Girling dampers.
Frame: Duplex tube cradle with 2·5-in diameter spine.
Dimensions: Wheelbase, 57·5 in; seat height, 32 in; ground clearance, 7·5 in; handlebar width, 26 in; castor angle, 62°; trail, 4·5 in; all unladen.
Weight: 448 lb, including one gallon of fuel.
Fuel Capacity: 4·8 gals including 4·8 pts reserve.
Oil Tank Capacity: 4·8 pts.
Manufacturer: Meriden Motorcycles Ltd, Meriden Works, Allesley, Coventry, Warwicks.

Performance

Maximum Speeds (Mean): 112·4 mph; 96·6 mph with rider in two-piece suit sitting normally.
Best One-way Speed: 116·3 mph — dry track, slight three-quarter tail wind.
Braking Distance — from 30 mph: 30 ft 4 in.
Fuel Consumption: 38·3 gals.
Oil Consumption: negligible.
Minimum Non-snatch Speed: 18 mph in top gear.
Speedo Accuracy:

Indicated mph	30	40	50	60	70	80	90
Actual mph	29·6	39·9	50·1	59·9	69·6	79·3	89

was very little rain during the period of the test, but on the one-and-only rain-showery day (and it would be the one we picked to do the touring story!) they caused no worry.

The Triumph is really comfortable. The seat height of 32 inches might seem a little high, but is compensated for by giving the seat a narrow nose, so the rider can reach the ground without strain. However, the seat could do with being a couple of inches longer. If the rear face of the seat were to be vertical, instead of sloping forward at top, it would make all the difference when carrying a passenger.

Ideally, a footrest position about an inch or two more to the rear would have been better but this, of course, is dictated by the position of the gear pedal. The pedal is slightly too far in front of the rest, and upward changes were best made by moving the foot forward until the heel was pivoting on the footrest; it came as second nature after a while. It is an excellent gearchange,

K70 HS version fitted to the previous TR7RV a TT100.

The use of a K70 studded tire on the front w difficult to understand, too, and with 1,800 mil on the speedometer, the tread showed distin signs of ratcheting.

However, that did not seem to affect th handling, and the extent to which the mod could be laid over in complete confidence wa evidenced by the flat ground away on the centr stand extension pedal.

At low speed, the steering was rather heavy o first acquaintance, growing lighter as speed ros but the novelty of this soon wore off and thereafter, it was accepted as normal.

There is some vibration present, at som sectors of the range, but it would not be a true born Triumph if there were not. We have t confess that the Tiger was a whole lot smoothe at 70 mph than some Triumphs we have ridde

On the other hand, after putting it full-whac

through the timing traps for a 113 mph mean you realise there are more sophisticated models around. Take it above the 6,000 rpm mark, and you get the distinct impression that there is a lot of machinery clanking around.

All right, so there may be. But on most highways, the number of chances of whacking a bike up to 113 mph can be counted on the fingers on a boxing glove. In more conventional riding conditions, the Tiger 750 does very well.

This is one of ye olde-fashioned machines which does not have the nicety, or the complex-

ties, of an electric starter. The very long-shanked kick starter is more than adequate to spin the crankshaft over with little muscular effort.

For once, here was a Triumph which did not call for the morning ritual of freeing the clutch plates, and although it did appreciate closing of the air lever for the first few seconds, that could be opened again almost immediately.

The air lever is mounted, somewhat inconveniently, on the front face of the air cleaner box and it had the annoying habit of partly closing itself with the machine in use. Something else the factory might consider relocating is the re-setting knob of the trip odometer drum. This is shrouded by the headlamp shell, and proved nigh-on impossible to operate without the expenditure of a large number of cuss-words.

On the credit side, there was nary a drip of oil on the garage floor in nearly three weeks of use; and the centre stand was one of the best we have come across, requiring just a flick of the toe to

hoist the model at almost the centre-point of balance, making access to either wheel a simple matter.

Another good point was the speedometer – when checked against MIRA's electronic timing gear it proved to be spot-on accurate, all the way up to the top of the scale. So, ninety on the clock really was ninety, with nothing added for rider flattery.

A fast, night-time run through the twisty lanes of the upper Teme Valley showed the effectiveness of the 45-watt main headlamp filament and, on switching to the motorway, a 70 mph after-dark cruising speed was held with ease.

The green 'main beam' indicator lamp in the top face of the headlamp shell was too bright and distracting, which sorely tempts you to cover up this new-fangled nonsense with a strip of sticking plaster.

And that, really, is about all that there is to say. The TR7RV Tiger 750 is a Triumph in the traditional style – lively, gutsy, tractable, and with the handling bred of a whole basket-full of production race victories.

If, performance-wise, it works out at just about on a par with the Bonnie, then that's the Bonnie's hard luck. Why have two carbs, when you can do it all with one?

Rear wheel of the Triumph Tiger is no longer the fabled quick release unit but a built-up hub with a disc brake

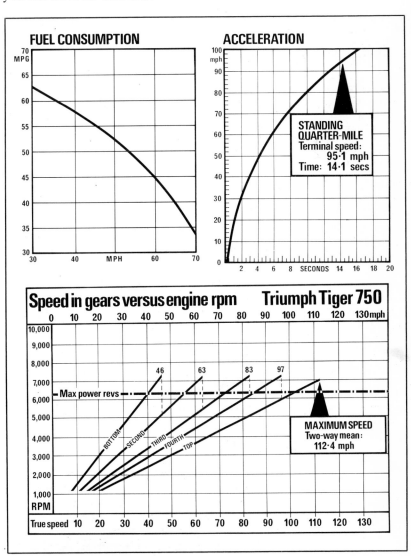

Yamaha XS750

In these days of increasing conformity in motor cycle designs from Japan, Yamaha's double overhead camshaft XS750 triple is something of a rarity – a bike of distinctive character and class with an extremely competitive price tag. Furthermore, it is a mature motor cycle. Yamaha could have very easily been drawn into the speed race that gripped the 750 cc roadster class in 1977. Instead, the XS750 is uniquely appealing for its flexibility, riding comfort and highly sophisticated equipment.

Should its specification, which includes a tough shaft drive, cast-alloy wheels and three

disc brakes, two on the front, one on the rear, sound like the perfect touring bike, then that is just a bonus in the deal. The XS750 can still give a good account of itself. Top speed approaches 120 mph and it can easily cruise at over 100 mph.

With that sort of performance it does not make the bike sensitive to constant maintenance. The shaft drive precludes chain tensioning and a typical neat touch is the use of rubber boots over the control levers to keep out water. However, the engine unit itself is enough to stand out in a crowd. Displacing 747 cc with an almost square bore and stroke of 68 by 68·6 mm and with the

o overhead cams chain driven from the left-
nd end of the crankshaft it has its three throws
 at 120 degrees like the now defunct Triumph
ident. The exhaust gives off the same rorty,
rbling note from the two silencers.
Only a light pull is needed to open up the three
-mm choke constant-velocity carburettors
d the engine immediately sets to the task. The
wer band is broad and full and although it
aks out at a maximum of 64 bhp at 7,500 rpm
ere is never any real need to approach this for
st riding. There is more than enough urge up to
00 rpm and, better still, with plenty of flywheel
rtia on the crankshaft you do not get any of
e annoying lurching between gear changes so
miliar on the bigger fours.
Inevitably, with the more direct drive between

the crankshaft and rear wheel resulting from a
Morse-type primary chain to the clutch and a
set of spur and bevel gears to the shaft from the
five-speed gearbox, the gear change is a lot less
crisp than on other, chain-drive Yamahas. But it
is still better, particularly in the lower ratios, than
the BMW gearbox with its mainshaft running at
higher speed.
Despite the 7,500 rpm rev-counter red line, the
Yamaha spins smoothly to 8,000 rpm through
the gears for maximum acceleration. But with an
all-up weight of 553 lb with the 4·5-gallon tank
full, it is hardly surprising that the flat out
acceleration is less potent than most seven fifties.
The standing quarter-mile time of 14·1 sec is
about seven tenths down on the best in the class
but on a par with the 750 cc BMW. Even so, the

*Rapidly becoming a
classic in enthusiast
motor cycling circles, the
Yamaha XS750 has a
double overhead
camshaft three-cylinder
engine and shaft drive,
plus an uncommonly
mature approach to
design features that
riders really need*

Specification

Engine: 747 cc (68 × 68·6 mm) double-overhead camshaft transverse, in-line three. Four plain main bearings; plain big ends. Wet sump lubrication with trochoid pump and replaceable oil filter. Compression ratio, 8·5 to 1. Three 34-mm choke Mikuni CV carburettors with lever-operated cold-start jets; oil-soaked foam air filter. Claimed maximum power, 64 bhp at 7,200 rpm. Maximum torque, 46 lb-ft at 6,000 rpm.

Transmission: Primary drive by inverted-tooth Morse Hy-vo chain. Wet, multiplate clutch and five-speed gearbox. Overall ratios: 13·29, 8·64, 7·07, 5·96 and 5·2 to 1. Final drive by spur and bevel gears and cardan shaft. Mph at 1,000 rpm in top gear, 14·5.

Electrical Equipment: Coil ignition. 12-volt, 14-amp-hour battery and 225-watt alternator. 7-in diameter with 45/50-watt sealed beam unit. Starter motor; four fuses; self-cancelling indicators.

Brakes: Hydraulically-operated 10·4-in diameter double-disc front, single-disc rear.

Tires: Bridgestone, 3·25H19 ribbed front, 4·00H18 patterned rear studded; Avon Roadrunners, 4·10H19 front, 4·25/85H18 rear on test machine. Yamaha cast-alloy seven spoke wheels.

Suspension: Kayaba telescopic front fork. Pivoted rear fork with five-position spring preload adjustment.

Frame: Duplex tube cradle-type with pressed-steel gusseting.

Dimensions: Wheelbase, 58·75 in; seat height, 33 in; ground clearance, 7 in; handlebar width, 27 in; trail, 4·5 in; castor angle, 63°; turning circle, 15 ft 6 in; all unladen.

Weight: 531 lb including one gallon of fuel.

Fuel Capacity: 4·5 gals. Vacuum-controlled taps.

Sump Oil Capacity: 7·8 pts.

Manufacturer: Yamaha Motor Co Ltd, 2500 Shingai, Shizuoka-ken, Tokyo.

Performance

Maximum Speeds (Mean): 117·1 mph; 104·2 mph with rider sitting normally.
Best One-way Speed: 122·3 mph — dry track, three-quarter tail wind.
Braking Distance – from 30 mph: 28 ft 3 in.
Fuel Consumption: 34 mpg overall.
Oil Consumption: Negligible.
Minimum Non-snatch Speed: 14 mph in top gear.
Speedo Accuracy:

Indicated mph	30	50	70	90
Actual mph	31·0	49·8	69·9	90·4

zero to 60 mph time of 6 sec gives the rider ple[n] to play with on the road. And with plenty of l[ow] end power the pick up from low speeds is m[ore] deceptive than the more highly tuned model[s].

The weight of the Yamaha may have produc[ed] its apparent thirst for fuel. The overall figure [we] returned was 34 mpg during the test but this [in]cluded a large proportion of motorway travelli[ng]. More typical may be the 41·6 mpg we obtained [on] one cross country run and the average 37·5 m[pg] obtained from a bike equipped with a full fairi[ng] in a 5,000 mile run across North America.

As a touring machine, there are few bikes [much] better the XS750, even among higher-pric[ed] models.

Riding comfort is excellent despite the hig[h] frequency buzz that the engine emits above 5,0[00] rpm. The dual seat is deeply padded and t[he] rubber-mounted handlebar is given just the rig[ht] amount of sweep at the grips for a balanced le[an] into the wind at over 70 mph. The depth of t[he] seat padding makes it very high at 33 in and th[is] might be awkward for shorter riders trying [to] balance the bike when stationary. But the heig[ht] of the seat lessens the possibility of cramping t[he] legs on a long run and gives a similar layout t[o] the BMW.

The test machine, which had 3,000 mile[s] clocked when collected, was fitted with Avo[n] Roadrunner tires in 4.10H19 and 4.25/85H1[8] sizes as replacements for the standard Bridg[e]stones. The British covers suited the bik[e] admirably.

Steering is neutral and precise and the bik[e] never needed anything more than a nod from th[e]

Setting a new fashion in superbike design is the shaft drive and supple suspension of the Yamaha three

er to whistle steadily through fast corners.
Suspension, in keeping with the touring image,
soft and remarkably compliant at speeds below
mph where it is in fact better than a BMW.
e front fork sliders have stick-free Teflon
shes that prevent the transmission of small
mps and ripples. A measure of their effective-
ss is that even running across a series of lane
rking studs on the motorway, the ride was
ver anything less than perfectly smooth.

The price you pay for such superlative riding
mfort is indifferent high speed handling in
nds. The rear suspension has slack damping
t produced a slow pitching in corners above
mph, and lighter riders reported a slight weave
a straight line above speeds of 100 mph.

An advantage of the Avon front tire was that
slightly larger diameter made the speedometer
ot-on accurate to 100 mph.

Braking is provided by three 10¼-in diameter
inless-steel discs with floating calipers. As on
evious Yamahas, the front double disc brake
eds a hard pull on the hand lever, but the rider
rewarded with progressive power.

The rear wheel also suffered from hopping if
e brake pedal was stamped on imprudently
en pulling up from high speed. The 28 ft 3 in
opping distance from 30 mph is more a
lection of the grippiness of the tires than the
wer of the brakes.

Apart from the 50/40-watt sealed beam Stan-
headlamp, which with its broad spread is only
erage in power, the electrics are otherwise
cellent.

Lamps and instruments are big and bright and
e self-cancelling indicators are a positive safety
vantage. Firing up on the electric starter never
led. The fuel taps are operated by the vacuum
om the outer two inlet tracts.

Not content with building one of the better all-
und motor cycles on the road, Yamaha have
ne a stage further and eased maintenance
sks.

An eighteen-piece toolkit includes Allen keys
r all the engine covers and there is even a loop
cable to compress the rear suspension to aid
ar wheel removal.

One additional convenience is that the rear
lf of the rear mudguard hinges up to aid wheel
moval – but why are other factories not
pable of offering it?

The Yamaha XS750 leaves the rider with the
easing impression that he has been thought of
hen the bike was conceived; that the test riders
overed a lot of miles when putting it through its
aces and that the designers expected the bike to
e more than just a flash in the pan.

How right they are; the bike is already very
opular with the touring rider and for 1978
ould satisfy those who want more power too.
amshafts with higher lift and more overlap plus
capacitor-discharge ignition that further re-
ces the Yamaha's limited maintenance, gives a
rformance more in line with the other Japanese
ven fifties.

Even now, the XS750 looks set to be a classic.

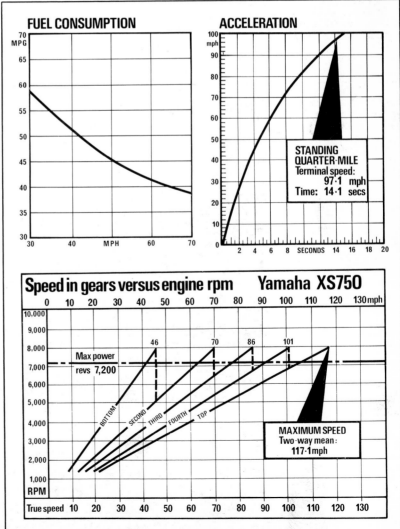

FUEL CONSUMPTION

ACCELERATION

STANDING
QUARTER-MILE
Terminal speed:
97·1 mph
Time: 14·1 secs

Speed in gears versus engine rpm   Yamaha XS750

Max power
revs 7,200

MAXIMUM SPEED
Two-way mean:
117·1 mph

Summarised Performance Data

Model	Capacity (cc)	Bore × Stroke (mm)	Engine Type	Max Power (bhp at rpm)	Weight (lb)	Max Speed (mph)	Standing Start ¼-Mile (sec at mph)	Overall Fuel Consumpt (mpg)
BMW R100RS	980	94 × 70·6	flat-twin	70 at 7,250	511	113·8	14·25 at 95·6	36·8
Ducati 860 GTS	864	86 × 74·4	vee-twin	67·7 at 7,000	520	114·9	13·85 at 97·0	35·9
Harley-Davidson FXE-1200	1,207	87·3 × 100·8	vee-twin	65·9 at 5,500	585	108·3	15·3 at 90·3	31·7
Harley-Davidson XLCR-1000	997·5	81 × 96·8	vee-twin	61 at 6,200	520	115·0*	13·5 at 102·0	37·5*
Honda CB750F2	736	61 × 63	transverse four	70 at 9,500	515	124·6	13·5 at 101·6	37·7
Honda Gold Wing GL1000	1,000	72 × 61·4	flat-four	80 at 7,500	616	124·6	13·2 at 103·7	34·6
Kawasaki Z650	652	62 × 54	transverse four	64 at 8,500	495	119·6	12·9 at 101·6	38·7
Kawasaki 750H2	748	71 × 63	transverse three‡	74 at 6,800	432	115·0	13·3 at 100·0	27·5†
Kawasaki Z1000	1,015	70 × 66	transverse four	83 at 8,000	550	124·4	12·65 at 105·5	35·8
Laverda 750SF	744	80 × 74	parallel twin	65 at 7,000	500	117·5	13·8 at 96·0	48·3†
Laverda Jota 1000	981	75 × 74	transverse three	90 at 7,600	522	137·8	13·05 at 111·55	35·4
Moto Guzzi Le Mans 850	844	83 × 78	vee-twin	80 at 7,300	485	123·4	14·0 at 98·9	33·0
MV Agusta 750S America	790	67 × 56	transverse four	75 at 8,500	510	120·2	13·8 at 100·2	38·4
Norton Commando 850 Mk 3	828	77 × 89	parallel twin	58 at 5,900	486	114·9	14·4 at 93·4	36·0
Suzuki GT750M	738	70 × 64	transverse three‡	70 at 6,500	550	119·8	13·5 at 99·5	37·7
Suzuki RE5	497‡‡	—	rotary	62 at 6,500	560	110·0	14·2 at 91·5	33·3
Suzuki GS750	749	65 × 56·4	transverse four	68 at 8,500	510	124·3	13·25 at 103·5	38·9
Triumph Trident T160	740	67 × 70	transverse three	58 at 7,250	518	119·5	13·8 at 97·8	31·3
Triumph TR7RV Tiger 750	744	76 × 82	parallel twin	46 at 6,200	448	112·4	14·1 at 95·1	38·3
Yamaha XS750	747	68 × 68·6	transverse three	64 at 7,500	531	117·1	14·1 at 97·1	34·0

* estimated.
† at 60 mph.
‡ two-stroke.
‡‡ chamber volume.

Index